DELICIOUS FISH

Claire Macdonald's inspired cooking at Kinloch Lodge Hotel on the Isle of Skye has made the restaurant one of the most celebrated in the country.

She was winner of the Glenfiddich Award for Cookery Writer of the Year in 1982, has been a regular contributor to the *Scottish Field* and is a member of the Taste of Scotland advisory committee to the Scottish Tourist Board. She is the author of *Seasonal Cooking* and *Sweet Things*.

She is married to the High Chief of Clan Donald and is the mother of four children.

By the same author

SEASONAL COOKING
SWEET THINGS

CLAIRE MACDONALD
of Macdonald

Delicious Fish

HarperCollins*Publishers*

HarperCollins*Publishers*
77–85 Fulham Palace Road,
Hammersmith, London W6 8JB

This paperback edition 1995
3 5 7 9 8 6 4 2

Previously published in paperback by Grafton 1989
Reprinted three times

First published in Great Britain by
Grafton Books 1986

Copyright © Claire Macdonald 1986

The Author asserts the moral right to
be identified as the author of this work

ISBN 0 586 20624 8

Set in Electra

Printed and bound in Great Britain by
Caledonian International Book Manufacturing Ltd, Glasgow

To my sisters and brothers-in-law,
Camilla and Jeremy
and
Olivia and Anthony

C·O·N·T·E·N·T·S

A·C·K·N·O·W·L·E·D·G·E·M·E·N·T·S

I would like to thank my family and several close friends for their help and patience while I got the recipes together and wrote the book, namely, Godfrey, my long-suffering husband; my mother, Jean Cathow; and my great friends who are an endless source of help and encouragement when it comes to inspiration – Peter Macpherson, Araminta Dallmeyer, Charlotte Donaldson, Lucy Baillie, Isobel Sydney, Sue London, my cousin Judith Coleridge, Caroline Fox, Angela Fox and Wendy Stephen. Last but not least my sisters Camilla and Olivia and their husbands Jeremy Westwood and Anthony Milburn.

I·N·T·R·O·D·U·C·T·I·O·N

Until recently fish had the worst reputation of all the food we eat. The treatment of fish in most institutions was largely responsible for this, and memories of fish school dinners took a long time to fade – until they were eradicated by a thoroughly delicious meal with fish as its main attraction.

Today the whole scene has changed. We are constantly told to eat less meat and more fish, for the sake of our health, and fish is now far more widely available and more attractively presented. Although I like meat, were I given the choice I would choose fish every time, not because it is better for me but because it appeals to me so much more than meat. And I'm not unusual in this. When we have fish on the menu at Kinloch Lodge, our home on Skye which is also a small hotel, our guests choose fish nine times out of ten, whether it is served as a first course – smoked fish pâté or mousse, soup or shellfish – or as a main course – trout, salmon, turbot or halibut with appropriately enhancing sauces. Far from being the second-rate item it used to be, fish now takes pride of place on the menu, even above our superb Scottish beef, game and venison.

Fish is so versatile. I experiment endlessly on our family (luckily all four of our children love fish!) and a fish pie, for instance, which some people regard as dismal, is for us a five-star dish which can be dressed up by adding a few prawns, or made even more appealing to children by covering the mashed potato topping with a generous layer of crushed potato crisps. Fish soups are always greeted with cries of glee, and one made with smoked haddock is my daughter Isabella's favourite food.

As we live on Skye, surrounded by water, you may suppose that we have always had ready access to a reliable and varied supply of fish. This is far from the case. All the fish caught in the waters around us used to be shipped direct to London. But during the last five years or so I have been lucky to find a sympathetic fish merchant in Mallaig, across on the mainland from us. He is called George Lawrie, and he supplies us with wonderful fresh fish. He also smokes his own kippers and haddock. After a telephone call from me, George gives my order to the ferry men, who in turn put it on the bus, which drops it off at the top of our road for us to collect, so fresh it's still almost flapping. There is also fish supplied by van, which delivers around the houses on Skye.

The demand for fish grows greater each year. Apart from the thriving fishmongers to be found in cities and towns – more are appearing all the time – the large supermarkets are all opening wet fish departments; although they have yet to grow as large as the butchery sections.

I really admire the fishermen who catch the fish we eat. Their way of life is as hard as any I can think of. Without wanting to sound melodramatic, they really do face danger all the time in their comparatively small boats on seas that can blow up suddenly into tremendous storms. When I think of the risks they take I never grudge the price I pay for fish.

I hope in this book to dispel the hang-ups people have in dealing with fish. Gutting and filleting are both very easy jobs provided that you have a *really* sharp knife. The gutting, too, is much cleaner than people suppose, done under a running cold tap. Fish live in seas and rivers and are clean eaters, so there is nothing disgusting about what you find inside them. In any case, if you can't face it, the fishmonger will do it for you. (If he doesn't offer without being asked, take your custom elsewhere.)

Cooking, as I do, virtually every day both for our guests (sort of dinner-party cooking) and for our family, I'm always experimenting with flavour combinations. It is surprising how cider, orange, bacon, nutmeg and even whisky can enhance both fish and shellfish.

I do hope that if you read this book you will find many recipes that make your mouth water so much you can't wait to buy some fish and start cooking. Good eating!

C·H·O·O·S·I·N·G F·R·E·S·H F·I·S·H

Ideally, if you can't catch your own (and that would reduce the number of fish eaters in Britain drastically) the best way to ensure a choice of really fresh fish is to hunt around for a good fish shop, and to get to know the owners and people who help in the shop really well. This will be no hardship if you love fish as I do.

Fresh fish can be distinguished by its appearance. A fish which is past the first flush of freshness has eyes which appear to have shrunk in their sockets, and the eyes look dull, not bright as they should be. The flesh looks dull, too, and the fish look limp instead of firm.

If you have your fish cleaned and filleted for you, remember to ask for the skins, heads and bones – invaluable for making fish stock.

Fresh fish that is to be used in a made-up dish such as a fish lasagne or a casserole can be kept in the fridge overnight and cooked the following day. But fish that is to be eaten grilled is best eaten on the same day, or frozen until needed. Smoked fish, of course, keeps better – 3–5 days in the fridge. Shellfish should always be eaten on the day of purchase.

E·Q·U·I·P·M·E·N·T U·S·E·F·U·L F·O·R F·I·S·H C·O·O·K·I·N·G A·N·D S·E·R·V·I·N·G

Even if, like many other people, you discover you and your family are eating more and more fish, it is unlikely that you will want to re-equip your kitchen specially for fish cookery. Fortunately it isn't necessary; standard equipment, as you will see from the list below, is quite adequate. A possible exception is the fish kettle. The price of buying one new would send you running to the butcher's for several pounds of Aberdeen Angus fillet. But if you can come by one, perhaps in a saleroom, grab the chance, because they can be very useful. Inside they have a tray with holes in, with handles at either end, which enable you to lift a large piece of fish out of the kettle, at the same time letting the liquid the fish cooked in drain back. This balancing act can be done if the fish has been cooked in an ordinary pan, by using two fish slices but they are often not strong enough to lift a fish, or a piece of fish, of any size, and the whole thing can slip off and splash back into the hot liquid. If you don't go in for cooking whole fish the following items are all you need:

Two fish slices: for turning and lifting

Large metal perforated spoon: for scooping and draining

Large frying pan: very useful for cooking several fish at one time, otherwise you will be frying trout, mackerel, etc., in relays

Small wire whisk: for whisking sauces

Extremely sharp filleting knife (or better still two): for when you do your own gutting and filleting

Sandwich tongs: for handling smaller fish like sardines, and also very useful for barbecuing fish

Basting brush: to be kept especially for fish so you won't worry about transmitting fishy flavours to other foods

Serving dishes: I like a selection of wide, shallow dishes for serving fish, either white glazed china, or brown earthenware. Very large platters suitable for serving whole salmon can still be picked up quite cheaply in old house sales, or in salerooms

A friend recently told me she had bought a large mirror for serving whole salmon on. I can imagine how striking it would look, as the centrepiece for a buffet party, but I haven't tried out the idea myself yet.

Small white glazed round dishes with an 'ear' at each side and a set of ramekins are invaluable for serving fishy first courses.

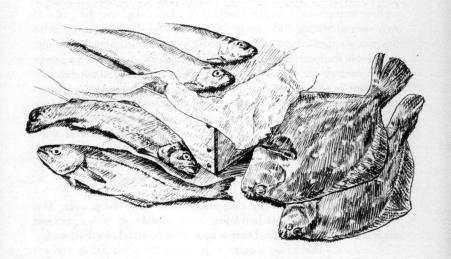

A·B·O·U·T F·I·S·H

I would like to dedicate this chapter to George Lawrie of Mallaig. George is our fish merchant and he supplies us with the wonderful fish and shellfish we have on the menu here at Kinloch. Before I started to write this chapter I went over to Mallaig and George spent a morning showing me round his fish-processing plant and telling me about fish, shellfish, smoking, salting, etc. One of the most impressive and endearing things about George Lawrie is that he bubbles over with enthusiasm when talking about fish. He appears to love his job, which like ours is really a way of life. And he loves cooking and eating fish of all sorts. He seems to have the same tastes as I do. When he was describing how he loves squid, cut in rings and cooked very quickly in olive oil and garlic, my mouth was watering at the very thought of it.

CLEANING AND FILLETING FISH

The most important item for easy filleting is a really sharp knife. This should not be the usual kitchen knife, but if possible one with a narrower blade called a boning knife. There is no need to be afraid of a sharp knife – it's blunt ones that cause accidents. Just hold the knife firmly and cut decisively.

To fillet a flat fish cut down either side of the backbone, working towards the outer sides, and keeping as close to the bones as you can. There is no need to gut a flat fish first.

To fillet a round fish such as a salmon gut it first, by cutting up its belly in a straight line. Scoop out the innards and wash the cavity left under running cold water. Cut off the head and tail, then, grasping your very sharp knife firmly, cut down one side of the backbone down the bones, very carefully so as not to leave behind any more flesh than you can help. When you have one side off repeat the process on the other side. Then, with the fish skin side down on the work surface, cut the skin off, by stroking the knife blade on it, held horizontally. This way you will get a skinned fillet of fish with no flesh whatever on the skin.

The first time you skin and fillet a fish it seems to take an age, but the more you do it the easier it becomes.

For the most part, fish is bought ready filleted and skinned, if you want. These tips are for those of you who, like me, have access to fresh fish in their natural state.

If you are filleting a big fish, like a turbot or a halibut, cut out the cheeks, as there is a good chunk of meat to be found there.

With fish to be eaten whole and unskinned, remove any scales by scraping them gently from tail to head, under running water.

FREEZING

George Lawrie says, and I agree with him, that contrary to what a lot of books say fish can be kept in the deep freeze for much longer than the usual given number of months. For example, fatty fish, like salmon, are usually given a life-span for edibleness of 3–6 months, whereas in my experience they are just as delicious after 9–12 months, providing they are frozen like this: gut the fish and freeze it unwrapped. When it is frozen hard, take it out of the deep freeze and dip it in water. Then wrap it and replace it in the freezer. George calls this glazing; it apparently prevents the natural dehydration of all foods while they are kept frozen, so you can do the same with meat. If you like, and George does, dip the fish more than once in water to increase the glaze.

SMOKING

HOT SMOKE

In hot smoking the fish are lightly cooked and have a strong smoky flavour. Hot-smoked fish, for example, mackerel, trout and Arbroath smokies, are ready to eat without further cooking. Arbroath smokies are herring which have been gutted and cleaned, but left round, not split. They are traditionally smoked hung in pairs on a stick by their tails, over logs in a pit.

Sometimes mackerel are smoked with a covering of crushed black peppercorns, which I find delicious. George has experimented with other spices and herbs on smoked fish, but nothing has been as popular as the peppercorns. Hot-smoked fish are smoked over oak sawdust, like cold-smoked fish. George Lawrie gets his oak shavings from the Cooperage in Edinburgh. Sometimes fish are both cold- and hot-smoked – like buckling. Buckling are herring which have been cleaned, then hung by their heads on sticks and cold-smoked for the first two hours, to dry the skin, then hot-smoked inside their dried skins. They are succulent and delicious eaten with lemon wedges and brown bread and butter.

COLD SMOKE

In cold smoking, the temperature is lower and the fish are not cooked at all. Cold-smoked fish include salmon (which is eaten raw), herring (kippers), haddock and whiting.

Traditionally smoking takes place in a smoke house, less traditionally in a vast smoking machine, which can be used for both cold and hot smoking. George Lawrie has both and says that he gets equally good results from the machine as he does from the smoke house, but that is only because he knows the quality he is aiming for, from the results from his smoke house. Sadly, there aren't many fish merchants who kipper in the traditional way. George's son is the fourth generation Lawrie who is versed in the arts of smoking, as, although it was George and his brother who founded the fish business, both their father and grandfather were smokers.

Every fish smoker has his own variations on how to prepare salmon for smoking. George spreads a mixture of salt, olive oil, demerara sugar and dark rum over his sides of salmon, leaves them for 19–20 hours, then smokes them overnight. Smoked salmon should be pale golden-pink in colour, and is traditionally served with brown bread and butter and lemon wedges. I like it served with brown bread and walnut rolls (rec. 78) or in the Jewish way, with cream cheese and bagels.

Smoked herring – kippers – are herring which have been split open and cleaned, then dipped for 20 minutes in a brine consisting of a 90% salt solution, then hung by their heads in pairs on a stick, placed on a rack and cold-smoked overnight. There are few things as delicious as a good kipper, and we think that George Lawrie's kippers are the finest in Britain. There are other contestants for this accolade: Loch Fyne kippers, Craster kippers, and Isle of Man kippers are all superb. Kippers can be cooked either under a grill, or (the method I like best) poached in a shallow pan of gently simmering water.

White fish which are to be smoked, such as haddock or whiting, are only dipped in brine for three minutes, because they are not oily like herring.

SALTING

The fish which comes immediately to mind when I think of salting is herring. My husband Godfrey and I both love salt herring – there is something very satisfying about salt herring and plain boiled potatoes. The only snag is that after a meal of salt herring come several hours of thirst, to be quenched by glass after glass of water. This thirst seems inevitable, no matter how long the herring are soaked before they are cooked or how many times the water is changed during cooking.

Salt herring are first cleaned, but their roes are left in, then packed in layers with salt in a wooden barrel. In the side of the barrel there is a bung. After three or four days of salting, this is removed, brine is poured in and the barrel is resealed. This is done because, as the salt dissolves in the juices which seep from the fish, the level drops, leaving an air space in which bacteria could breed. The barrel is then turned from time to time. Salt herring is ready to be eaten after seven days.

A red herring is not just the proverbial distraction, but one which has just spawned. These fish have a slit cut in their necks, but are otherwise left whole and uncleaned. They are then salted, as for ordinary salt herring. When they are to be smoked, they are soaked overnight in fresh water, then hung at the top of the smoke house for a whole month. You have to really love the salty smoky flavour to enjoy red herring!

DRIED FISH

Fish isn't really dried to any great extent in this country. Fish to be dried are cleaned and washed in salty water, then hung outside with a cover over them. Ideally the day they are dried should be a bright, windy day, with the wind being preferably from the north. Dried fish don't need to be stored in refrigeration, and the goodness in them lasts for a couple of years.

SQUID

Squid are delicious and not as difficult to clean as people think. Inside the body there is a feather-shaped blade of cartilage. If you grasp this firmly and pull it comes out. Throw away head, innards and ink sac. Then wash the squid well in running water both inside and out and cut it into circles, reducing the tentacles to 4 cm (1½ inch) lengths. The thing to remember not to do with squid is to overcook it – a minute or two in olive oil and garlic is all it needs. If squid is left cooking for too long it becomes tough and very chewy – rather like overcooked liver or kidney.

SHELLFISH

SCALLOPS

We buy our scallops shelled. But if you happen to get them still in their shells, don't be daunted by the thought of prizing them loose, because there is a very quick and easy method, as shown me by George Lawrie. Hold the scallop with the flat shell against the palm of your hand. Stick a long thin knife into the 'waist' of the shell, and cut firmly round – the meat will be left in the rounded shell. Remove the frilly bit round the very edges of the white meat, and the little dark grey tube at the side of the coral. There is your scallop, ready to cook.

MUSSELS

We have quantities of mussels growing on the rocks below our house, just there for the picking. We leave them overnight in a bucket of fresh water with a couple of handfuls of oatmeal. This is supposed to be eaten by the mussels which then rid themselves of any grit inside their stomachs. I'm never quite sure if they really do this but we give them the opportunity. Then the mussels need to be scrubbed well, under running water.

To cook put them in a large saucepan which has a tightly fitting lid, and add white wine (how much depends on how many mussels), an equal quantity of water, a small onion, very finely chopped, and a handful of chopped parsley. Cover the pan and put over a moderately high heat, shaking it from time to time, for 7–10 minutes. Throw out any mussels

which aren't open – these will have been dead before they were cooked, and so aren't safe to eat.

PRAWNS

The huge, succulent Dublin Bay prawns which we are lucky enough to get are also known as Norwegian lobsters. When they have their heads removed they can legitimately be called, under the Trades Descriptions Act, scampi tails. So, a prawn by any other name can only be a shrimp!

The answer to cooking all prawn-type shellfish is boiling water. Get a big pan of water boiling fast, then put your prawns in, and as soon as they float to the surface of the water they are cooked. Drain them at once. If they are at all overcooked they become mushy. To shell prawns wait until they are cool enough to handle, squeeze them lengthwise, then break apart their shells and the curved, cooked body can be pulled out.

LOBSTER

You pay more to eat lobster on menus throughout the world than any other item, and yet I personally much prefer crab, prawns and scallops – unless the lobster is really fresh. Lobster is so often tough and chewy, and I also think the flavour of crab and scallops is much nicer. But I know that I am very much in a minority.

Having said all that, I do love really fresh lobster, served simply, either cold with a good mayonnaise, or hot with melted butter, a squeeze of lemon juice and chopped chives.

To cook lobsters see recipe 123.

CRAB

I love crab, preferably eaten plain, with some good mayonnaise and brown bread. My husband loves both crab and lobster served hot, with rich sauces made with cream, brandy or cheese.

To cook crab, have ready a pan of boiling, salted water and plunge them in – this kills them instantly. Boil them for about 10–15 minutes to the half kilo or pound and cool them on a tray. To shell a crab, stand it on its head with its big claws down, and press at the top of the shell with both your thumbs. This opens the shell so you can pull the body and claws away. Throw away the bundle of intestines and scoop any soft, creamy brown flesh from inside the shell into a bowl. On the body of the crab are the gills, known repulsively as the dead man's fingers; pull these out. Scoop and scrape the flesh from the body, then, with a rolling pin or hammer, bash the claws and pick out the white meat inside. I like to mix the white and brown meat together, and here at Kinloch when we have fresh crab on the menu, I serve the crabmeat just like this, on a bed of shredded lettuce, with a Tomato and garlic mayonnaise (rec. 23) at the side.

OTHER FISH

Fish other than shellfish divides into categories in two ways. One way is by shape. There are, roughly speaking, two shapes of fish:

Round Fish, including such fish as salmon, cod, herring, haddock, mackerel, bass, whiting, trout, red mullet and grey mullet, and many others, and

Flat Fish, including turbot, sole, plaice, halibut and brill.

Another way of categorizing fish is by the texture of its flesh. There are soft fish such as plaice, lemon sole, grey sole and haddock (although haddock is slightly less soft in texture than the others). These fish require very careful cooking, as they tend to fall apart if they are overcooked.

Then there are firmer fleshed fish such as turbot and halibut (both of which are also fairly gelatinous in texture), Dover sole, skate, cod and monkfish (which is very firm-fleshed). These fish stand up to cooking much better than the softer fleshed variety. They are suitable for using as kebabs, in barbecuing, and for casseroling.

Some fish are much oilier than others – the one which immediately springs to mind is herring, which is also the most nutritious of all fish. Mackerel is also very oily, and so are salmon, pilchards and sardines, and swordfish.

FISH STOCK

This is well worth making. It doesn't take a minute to put together, and only 10 minutes to cook, but it makes such a difference to fish dishes.

In a saucepan, put 575 ml (1 pint) each of dry white wine and water, any fish skin and bones, an onion, skinned and sliced, a carrot, chopped, a bay leaf, a few stalks of parsley and about 12 peppercorns. Bring the liquid to the boil and simmer for 10 minutes. Pour the stock into whatever dish you are going to cook the fish in and leave to cool. Put the filleted fish into the stock and cover with greaseproof paper to cook.

If you are making a dish where stock is not required, such as roasted monkfish, don't waste the trimmings – make up a fish stock and freeze it for later use.

Certain fish – turbot and skate in particular – make a very gelatinous stock, which can be useful for cold fish dishes.

CHICKEN STOCK

It may sound odd, but some of the recipes in this book contain chicken stock. This is usually where tinned fish or preserved fish is used, like the Tuna and sweetcorn soup, or where the fish used, like the smoked salmon in the Smoked salmon mousse, doesn't give you anything with which to make fish stock. Home-made chicken stock is best, but if you have none available a stock cube will do. Or make up some vegetable stock: just boil up a chopped onion, skin and all, with some carrot and any other vegetables to hand except potato, for about an hour.

S·O·U·P·S

Creamy Smoked Haddock Soup
Salmon and Parsley Soup
Tuna and Sweetcorn Soup
Mussel and Onion Chowder
Crab and Rice Soup
Fishhead Soup
Moules Marinières
Kipper and Tomato Chowder
Bouillabaisse Écossaise
Prawn Bisque
Spinach, Yoghurt and Prawn Soup

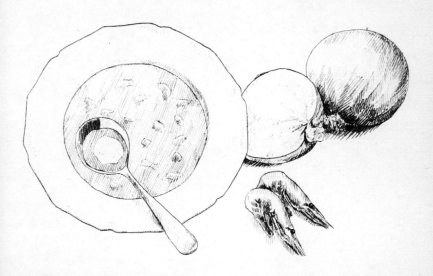

1 Creamy Smoked Haddock Soup

One of the best soups I know, this is extremely popular when we put it on the menu here at Kinloch.

Serves 6
700 g (1½ lb) smoked haddock
1.1 litres (2 pt) milk and water mixed
50 g (2 oz) butter
2 onions, skinned and chopped
3 medium potatoes, peeled and chopped
½ tsp freshly grated nutmeg
2 tomatoes, skinned, seeded and chopped
freshly ground black pepper
1 heaped tbsp finely chopped parsley
single cream to serve (optional)

Put the fish into a saucepan with the milk and water. Bring the liquid slowly to the boil and simmer for just 5 minutes, then remove the pan from the heat and let the fish cool in the liquid.

Melt the butter in another saucepan and add the onion. Cook over a moderate heat, stirring occasionally, for about 5 minutes, until it is soft and transparent. Then add the potato and cook for a further 5 minutes, stirring from time to time to prevent sticking. Strain in the liquid the fish cooked in and simmer gently for 30 minutes or until the potato is soft.

Remove the pan from the heat. Add the nutmeg and pepper and liquidize the soup until smooth. Flake the cooked fish into the soup, being careful to remove all bones and skin. Stir in the tomatoes and, just before serving, add the parsley.

Serve with a spoonful of cream in each plateful, if you like.

2 Salmon and Parsley Soup

This delicious soup is a good way of using up leftover salmon, and making a little go a long way.

Serves 6–8
175 g (6 oz) cooked salmon, flaked and with bones and skin removed
50 g (2 oz) butter
1 large onion, skinned and chopped
2 large potatoes, peeled and finely chopped
575 ml (1 pt) chicken stock
575 ml (1 pt) milk
freshly grated nutmeg
salt and black pepper
2 tbsp chopped parsley

Melt the butter in a saucepan over a moderate heat. Add the onion and cook, stirring from time to time, for about 5 minutes, until it is soft and transparent. Add the potato and cook for a further couple of minutes. Then pour on the stock and the milk, season with nutmeg, salt and pepper to taste, cover the pan with a lid and simmer gently for 30 minutes or until the potato is quite soft.

Remove from the heat, cool and liquidize together with the parsley. Flake the salmon into the smooth soup. Reheat to serve, but try not to let the soup sit over heat for too long, as the fresh green colour of the parsley tends to turn brown.

3 Tuna and Sweetcorn Soup

This is a very filling soup – ideal for lunch on a winter's day. It is one of the top favourites with our four children, and has the added bonus of being extremely quick and simple to put together.

Serves 6–8
50 g (2 oz) butter
50 g (2 oz) flour, wholemeal or plain
1 tbsp curry powder
1.1 litres (2 pt) milk and chicken stock mixed
2 × 335 g (11.8 oz) cans sweetcorn, drained
200 g (7 oz) can tuna fish, drained
salt and freshly ground black pepper
2 tbsp finely chopped parsley

Melt the butter in a saucepan and stir in the flour and curry powder. Cook, stirring, for a couple of minutes, then gradually add the milk and chicken stock, stirring continuously until it boils. Stir in the sweetcorn and tuna. Season to taste, sprinkle with parsley and serve hot.

4 *Mussel and Onion Chowder*

We are lucky in having rocks below our house covered with mussels just there for the picking. Onions and mussels seem to complement each other, and this is one of those soups which are almost a meal in themselves.

Serves 6–8
0.8 litre (1½ pt) mussels, well scrubbed under running water
125 ml (4 fl oz) dry white wine
1 onion, skinned and quartered
75 g (3 oz) butter
2 large or 3 medium onions, skinned and finely sliced
2 rounded tbsp flour
1.1 litres (2 pt) of the liquid in which the mussels cooked
1 tbsp finely chopped parsley
salt and freshly ground black pepper

First put the mussels in a large saucepan with 1.1 litres (2 pt) of water, the wine and onion quarters. Place over a high heat, cover the pan and cook for 10 minutes, shaking the pan occasionally. Remove from the heat and throw out any mussels which have not opened. Strain off and reserve the liquid. When the mussels are cool enough to handle, take them out of their shells and keep on one side.

Melt the butter in another saucepan, add the sliced onions and cook over a moderate heat, stirring, for 10 minutes. Then stir in the flour and gradually add the mussel liquid, stirring all the time until the mixture boils. Season with pepper and a little salt if you like.

Stir in the mussels and parsley and serve hot.

5 Crab and Rice Soup

We are very lucky to have a good supply of crab available to us here at Kinloch. However we are using it, we mix together the white and brown meat in even quantities. I generally prefer to eat crab cold, but it is very good in this hot soup.

Serves 6–8
50 g (2 oz) butter
1 large onion, very finely chopped
50 g (2 oz) long-grain white rice, preferably basmati
450 g (1 lb) crabmeat
1.1 litres (2 pt) milk and chicken stock, equally mixed
1 tbsp finely chopped parsley
salt and freshly ground black pepper
freshly grated nutmeg

Melt the butter in a large saucepan and add the onion. Cook for 5 minutes over a moderate heat, stirring occasionally, then add the rice. Cook for a further couple of minutes, then pour on the milk and stock. Simmer for 20–30 minutes, until the rice is cooked, then stir in the crabmeat and cook for a further 5 minutes. Season with salt, pepper and nutmeg to taste and sprinkle with parsley before serving.

6 Fishhead Soup

This may sound rather off-putting, but it tastes delicious, made from the fishheads which would usually be chucked in the bin. Fishhead soup is a traditional Scots dish and this is my version.

Serves 6–8
1 salmon head or 6 haddock heads
1.1 litres (2 pt) water
1 onion, skinned and quartered
a few peppercorns
1 carrot, peeled and chopped
For the soup
50 g (2 oz) butter
1 large onion, skinned and chopped
2 carrots, peeled and chopped
2 potatoes, peeled and chopped
1 stick of celery, chopped
the strained fishhead liquid
salt and freshly ground black pepper

First cook the fishhead(s). Put in a saucepan together with the water, onion, peppercorns and carrot and bring to the boil. Simmer gently for an hour, remove from the heat and strain.

To make the soup, melt the butter in a saucepan, add all the chopped vegetables, and cook for about 5 minutes over a moderate heat, stirring occasionally. Pour on the fishhead stock, cover and simmer for 30 minutes, until the vegetables are tender. Leave to cool.

Liquidize the soup, season to taste and reheat before serving.

7 *Moules Marinières*

Although it takes only a short time to cook, this soup takes a longer time to prepare, what with scrubbing the mussels. But it is worth every minute, and one of my favourites. Here are two versions, the first being a bit simpler than the second, which is more for a party or special occasion.

Serves 6–8
3.3 litres (6 pt) mussels
2 large garlic cloves, skinned and very finely chopped
freshly ground black pepper
0.8 litre (1½ pt) water
275 ml (½ pt) dry white wine
2 tbsp finely chopped parsley
3 egg yolks and 200 ml (7 fl oz) double cream to serve (optional)

Scrub each mussel under running cold water with a hard-bristled brush. Rinse well under cold water, then put them into a large saucepan together with the garlic, pepper, water and wine. Cover the pan and put on a high heat for 10 minutes, shaking it from time to time. Stir in the parsley and divide between soup plates. (Put a couple of spare plates on the table for discarded mussel shells.) Serve with brown wholemeal rolls or, better still but not so healthy, warm garlic bread dripping with butter!

The smarter version is cooked in the same way, but before serving strain the liquid off into another saucepan. Beat together the egg yolks and double cream. Stir some of the hot mussel liquid into this, then stir the cream mixture into the pan. Reheat, stirring, but do not boil. Put the mussels back into the soup and serve.

8 *Kipper and Tomato Chowder*

This is an unlikely sounding combination, but an unusual and delicious soup results from it. You can, if you like, liquidize and sieve it before serving, but I much prefer it with the bits of onion, tomato, potato and kipper.

Serves 6–8
50 g (2 oz) butter
2 medium onions, skinned and finely sliced
2 large potatoes, peeled and diced
2 × 425 g (15 oz) cans tomatoes
½ tsp sugar
salt and freshly ground black pepper
1 tsp dried basil, or 3–4 sprigs of fresh basil
575 ml (1 pt) water
2 large juicy kippers
finely chopped parsley to serve

Poach the kippers in water and leave to cool. Flake the flesh from the skins and remove as many of the bones as possible.

Melt the butter in a saucepan, add the onion and cook over a moderate heat for 5 minutes until it is soft and transparent, stirring occasionally. Add the potatoes, tomatoes, sugar, salt and pepper, basil and water and simmer for about 30 minutes. Crush the tomatoes against the sides of the pan to break them up, fishing out any cores you can spot.

When the potato is quite soft stir in the kipper meat. Serve with a sprinkling of parsley on each portion.

9 *Bouillabaisse Écossaise*

This isn't proper bouillabaisse, of course, because we are a long way from the Mediterranean and the fish to be found there. Actually I'm not at all sorry, because I think Mediterranean fish are pretty drab at the best of times, over-endowed with bones, and this fish soup is far nicer, made with the delicious fish caught in the chilly waters of the Atlantic Ocean or the North Sea. The fish is traditionally left on the bone for bouillabaisse, but I see no great virtue in a dish if while eating it one is constantly having to remove bones from one's mouth, so I use filleted fish.

Serves 6–8
4 tbsp olive oil
1 large onion, skinned and finely sliced
1.4 kg (3 lb) fish (a mixture of cod, fresh haddock and monkfish), cut into 5 cm (2 in) chunks
4 tomatoes, skinned, seeded and sliced or chopped
2 pinches of saffron
2 garlic cloves, skinned and finely chopped
some parsley stalks and a couple of sprigs of thyme
salt and freshly ground black pepper

Put the oil in a heavy-bottomed casserole and add the onion. Cook for about 5 minutes over a moderate heat, stirring occasionally, until the onion is transparent and soft. Then add the chunks of fish, tomatoes, saffron, garlic, parsley and thyme. Season and add enough water just to cover the fish. Bring to the boil and boil fast for 5 minutes, then more gently for a further 5 minutes.

Remove the parsley stalks and sprigs of thyme and ladle into soup plates. Serve with French bread and Tomato and garlic mayonnaise (rec. 23).

10 Prawn Bisque

A bisque, which can be made equally well with lobster or crab as with prawns, has a luxuriant ring to it. It conjures up a smooth, steaming soup of shellfish with brandy and cream playing quite a major role in the contents. It is actually a very good, very simple soup, and there doesn't need to be that much brandy or cream – just enough of both to make their presence felt.

Serves 6–8
450 g (1 lb) cooked, peeled prawns, shells reserved
1 onion, skinned and quartered
1 bouquet garni
575 ml (1 pt) water
275 ml (½ pt) dry white wine
50 g (2 oz) butter
2 rounded tbsp flour
275 ml (½ pt) milk and the strained liquid from the prawn shells
freshly grated nutmeg
salt and freshly ground black pepper
2 tbsp brandy
6–8 tbsp double cream
finely chopped parsley to serve

Put the onion, bouquet garni, water, wine and prawn shells into a saucepan, cover and bring to the boil. Simmer for about 45 minutes. Meanwhile chop the shrimps or prawns and set on one side.

Melt the butter in a saucepan, stir in the flour and cook for a minute or two, then gradually add the milk and strained prawn shell stock, stirring until the soup boils. Season with a little nutmeg and salt and pepper to taste. Stir in the chopped prawns and, just before serving, stir in the brandy.

Serve with a spoon of cream in the middle of each plateful, topped with finely chopped parsley.

11 Spinach, Yoghurt and Prawn Soup

The prawns in this soup are really just the garnish, so you can be as lavish or otherwise as you like.

Serves 6–8
50 g (2 oz) butter
2 medium onions, skinned and chopped
900 g (2 lb) frozen spinach, thawed and drained
rind of 1 lemon, pared off with a potato peeler
1 large garlic clove, skinned and chopped
1.1 litres (2 pt) chicken stock
salt and freshly ground black pepper
freshly grated nutmeg
6–8 tbsp natural yoghurt
175 g (6 oz) prawns or shrimps (if the prawns are very big, chop them)
lemon slices and/or chopped parsley to garnish (optional)

Melt the butter in a saucepan, add the onion and cook, stirring occasionally, for 5 minutes. Add the spinach, lemon rind, garlic, stock, salt, pepper and nutmeg. Simmer gently for 20 minutes, then cool a bit, liquidize and reheat. Serve with a spoonful of yoghurt on each plateful and the prawns divided evenly between them. Garnish, if you like, with a thin slice of lemon and/or a sprinkling of parsley.

B·R·E·A·K·F·A·S·T, B·R·U·N·C·H OR S·U·P·P·E·R D·I·S·H·E·S

Fishcakes
Smoked Haddock with Poached Eggs
Fried Oatmeal-coated Herring
Kedgeree
Grilled Mackerel with Gooseberry Sauce
Fried Cod's Roe with Apple Rings and Bacon
Omelette with Creamy Smoked Haddock and Tomato
Omelette with Prawns, Bacon and Parsley
Scrambled Eggs with Smoked Salmon
Devilled Herring Roes on Toast

Sadly, for most of us nowadays breakfast is a rushed meal usually involving not much more than a cup of coffee or tea and a piece of toast. But if you do have the time, perhaps at weekends, for a leisurely breakfast or brunch, the recipes in this chapter make delicious and ideal main dishes. Some of them, like the kedgeree and the fishcakes, can be made the previous day and just need to be heated up in the case of the kedgeree, or fried in the case of the fishcakes. Other recipes, like the mackerel, don't take very long to cook and would be ideal for a more hurried weekday breakfast. It always surprises me how our guests here at Kinloch all say that they can't eat any lunch after the large breakfasts they eat here, but just today I had a cooked breakfast and found myself quite unhungry at lunch and so I am determined to try and eat a cooked breakfast every day along with our children. It certainly kills the desire (which is strong in me!) to lick out bowls as I cook and sneak into the larder to eat bits off the leftovers from the previous evening! So it's taken me fifteen years to realize that eating a cooked breakfast might be the way to lose some weight. But of course all the recipes in this chapter can be eaten at any meal and they make equally good supper dishes as breakfast ones.

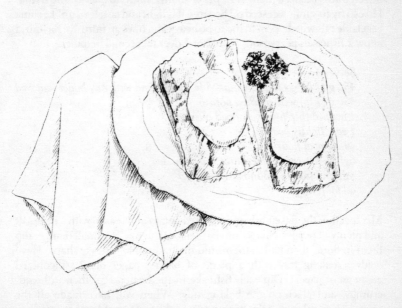

12 Fishcakes

Fishcakes are a very tasty way of using up leftovers, indeed so good that they are worth making even if you don't have any leftover fish. If I am making them from scratch I use smoked haddock which has been gently poached in milk and water for 4–5 minutes, cooled in its cooking liquid, then flaked from its skin. If I have any salmon left over, I make it up into delicious salmon fishcakes.

The secret of a good fishcake is to have equal quantities of fish and potato, and to make your own breadcrumbs – just slightly stale bread made into crumbs and lightly toasted – instead of using the bright orange bought ones, which are full of E102 and E110, the increasingly suspect orange and yellow dyes.

Fishcakes are extremely convenient because they can be made and frozen until you need them. They take about 2 hours to thaw before frying. I like to fry in sunflower seed oil because it is light and tasteless, unlike some vegetable oils which seem to me to be heavy and have an intrusive flavour. I allow 2 fishcakes per person, with 2 or 3 over for second helpings.

Serves 4
450 g (1 lb) cooked fish, flaked from skin and with any bones removed
450 g (1 lb) well-mashed potato
1 heaped tbsp finely chopped parsley
1 egg, lightly beaten
wholemeal flour
lightly toasted breadcrumbs, homemade
salt and freshly ground black pepper
oil for frying

Mix together the flaked fish and mashed potato and season with a little salt and plenty of pepper. Shape into balls about the size of a small orange, dip them in flour, then flatten them into the traditional fishcake shape. Have ready a baking tray with a piece of baking paper on it (siliconized greaseproof paper). Dip each fishcake in the beaten egg, then in bread-crumbs, and place on the baking tray. When you have made all the mixture into cakes, put the baking tray in the fridge until you are ready to fry them. If you want to freeze them, do so at this stage.

When you are ready to cook them, pour oil into a shallow pan or frying pan to a depth of about 6 mm (¼ in) and heat it. Fry the fishcakes until they are golden brown all over. Keep them warm in the oven on a dish lined with a couple of thicknesses of absorbent paper to remove any excess oil.

Fishcakes are very good served with grilled tomatoes, or with Fresh tomato sauce (rec. 29).

---

13 Smoked Haddock with Poached Eggs

Really good smoked haddock, plump, pale beige and delicious, is worth hunting out. Marks and Spencer sell very good pieces of filleted smoked haddock which are free of artificial colouring. Beware any bright orange smoked haddock – it has been saturated in dye.

This recipe doesn't take long at all to prepare – while the fish is gently cooking in the milk, the eggs can be poaching.

Serves 4
4 × 175 g (6 oz) pieces of smoked haddock
milk
4–8 eggs

Put 4 plates to warm. Place the fish in a saucepan, pour on just enough milk to cover it and put the pan on a moderate heat. Bring the milk to a gentle simmer, reduce the heat and cook for 4–5 minutes. Then draw the pan off the heat and leave the fish to finish cooking in the hot milk until you are ready to serve. Meanwhile poach the eggs.

I like to serve the smoked haddock in a pool of the milk in which it cooked, with warm brown rolls or bread to mop it up after you have eaten the fish and poached eggs.

14 Fried Oatmeal-coated Herring

It is hard to beat a really fresh herring, dipped in oatmeal and fried. It is one of my husband Godfrey's favourite foods, and mine too. I like them served with Mustard sauce (rec. 31).

Allow 1 herring per person. Cut off the heads and tails. Dip them in oatmeal, and fry them in sunflower oil for just 3–4 minutes on each side. Their delicate skins almost melt into the oatmeal, which becomes crispy. Serve immediately, with Mustard sauce if you like.

15 Kedgeree

Kedgeree is one of my favourite of all fish dishes. Like fish pie, it can be dreary; but it should be delicious. You can use smoked fish or leftover salmon. If I'm using smoked haddock, I use the milk and water in which I cook the fish to cook the rice in. If the kedgeree is made with leftover salmon and is to be eaten as a supper dish, it is very good served with hollandaise sauce.

Serves 6
225 g (8 oz) smoked haddock
1.1 litres (2 pt) of milk and water mixed
125 g (4 oz) butter
1 onion, skinned and finely chopped
225 g (8 oz) brown rice
2 hard-boiled eggs, shelled and chopped
1 heaped tbsp finely chopped parsley
freshly ground black pepper
pinch of ground mace (optional)

Put the smoked haddock in a saucepan with the milk and water. Place on a moderate heat and bring to a gentle simmer. Simmer for about 5 minutes, then draw the pan off the heat and let the fish cool for about 10 minutes in the liquid. Then strain the liquid into a jug. When the fish is cool enough to handle, flake it from the skin, removing any bones.

In another saucepan, melt half the butter. Add the finely chopped onion and cook for 5 minutes or so, stirring occasionally, until it is soft and transparent. Then add the rice and cook for a further 2 minutes, stirring once or twice. Pour on the strained fish liquid, bring to simmering point and cook for 30–40 minutes, until the rice is just cooked but still retains a slight nuttiness. Drain well, return the rice to the saucepan and heat gently, stirring, to dry it out a bit. Mix in the flaked fish, chopped hard-boiled eggs, parsley, pepper, and mace if using. Melt or finely dice the remaining butter and stir it through the kedgeree. Serve hot.

If the kedgeree is made to be reheated and served a few hours later, put it into an ovenproof dish and put in a moderate oven (180°C, 350°F, gas 4) for 30–40 minutes, forking the rice through a couple of times as it heats.

If you are using leftover cooked salmon for the kedgeree, and happen to have some chicken stock, cook the rice in it. Otherwise add a chicken stock cube to the water with the rice.

16 Grilled Mackerel with Gooseberry Sauce

Mackerel, especially the first of the season, are a great favourite of mine. They are very oily fish, so I like to grill them rather than fry them, and serve them with this sharp gooseberry sauce.

Allow 1 small to medium mackerel per person. Cut off their heads and tails and clean them under running water, then pat them dry with absorbent paper. Slash them diagonally about 3 times on each side, and put them in a tin under a moderate grill. Cook for 10–15 minutes on each side, then serve with gooseberry sauce.

Gooseberry sauce
450 g (1 lb) gooseberries
150 ml (¼ pt) water
25 g (1 oz) granulated sugar
freshly grated nutmeg

Put the gooseberries and water into a saucepan and cover. Cook over a moderate heat until the gooseberries are soft, then draw the pan off the heat and stir in the sugar and some freshly grated nutmeg. When cool liquidize until smooth – this is why you don't need to bother to top and tail the gooseberries before cooking.

17 Fried Cod's Roe with Apple Rings and Bacon

Bacon goes well with almost all fish and shellfish, and the combination of bacon, fried apple rings and cod roe is delicious.

Serves 1
2 × 1 cm (½ in) slices cod's roe
½ eating apple, ideally Granny Smith's or Cox's
1 tbsp lemon juice
2 bacon rashers
oil for frying

Peel and core the apple, and cut into thick slices. Keep them in a bowl of water with a tablespoon of lemon juice added to help prevent them from going brown. Before frying, pat the apple slices dry with absorbent paper.

Grill the bacon until crisp. Fry the slices of cod roe in a little oil until they are golden brown on each side. Keep them warm on a serving dish lined with absorbent paper to remove excess fat, in a cool oven. Then wipe the frying pan out, heat a little more oil in it, and fry the apple slices until they are just soft.

Serve all together, immediately – if the apple slices sit for any length of time keeping warm they tend to go flabby.

18 Omelette with Creamy Smoked Haddock and Tomato

This is a flat omelette, served with cooked, flaked smoked haddock in a creamy sauce, with chopped tomato and parsley – it looks as good as it tastes. The smoked haddock and tomato sauce can be made ahead of time, so that the final omelette-making is very quick. I like to serve them with our home-made granary bread.

Serves 4
450 g (1 lb) smoked haddock
0.8 litre (1½ pt) milk
50 g (2 oz) butter
2 tbsp flour
freshly ground black pepper
freshly grated nutmeg
2 tomatoes, skinned, seeded and chopped
1 heaped tbsp finely chopped parsley
8 eggs
butter for frying

Put the fish into a saucepan with the milk, place over a moderate heat and bring to a gentle simmer. Simmer for 5 minutes, then draw the pan off the heat and leave the fish to cool in the milk. Strain the milk into a jug and flake the fish off the skin, removing any bones.

Melt the butter in a saucepan and stir in the flour. Cook for a minute or two, stirring occasionally, then gradually add 575 ml (1 pt) of the milk the fish cooked in, stirring continuously until the sauce boils. Mix in the flaked fish, tomatoes, seasoning and parsley, and keep warm while you make the omelettes (as described in the following recipe).

If the sauce has been made in the morning, reheat gently until not quite simmering. Pour a quarter of it over the first omelette, and keep it warm while you make the second, adding more butter as necessary, until all 4 omelettes are made. I always keep the first omelette made for myself, the second for my husband Godfrey, and the last 2 for our guests, as they will be a bit better, obviously, than the first ones.

19 Omelette with Prawns, Bacon and Parsley

My parents live quite close to Morecambe Bay, where they get tiny, pink, peppery-tasting shrimps. If you can get them, I think they are just as good as prawns – and much better than some frozen prawns, which can be rather tasteless. This omelette is a luxurious one with its filling of prawns (or shrimps), chopped-up crisply cooked bacon, and parsley. The flavours combine together very well, and the crunch of the bacon gives a good contrast in texture.

Serves 4
8 eggs
4 tbsp water
salt and freshly ground black pepper
hot pepper sauce (Tabasco)
25–50 g (1–2 oz) butter
For the filling
8 bacon rashers, grilled until crisp, drained on absorbent paper, then broken into bits
225 g (8 oz) peeled, cooked prawns (or shrimps)
1 heaped tbsp finely chopped parsley

Mix the filling ingredients together.

For each omelette, break 2 eggs into a bowl, add 1 tbsp water, a little salt and pepper and a dash of hot pepper sauce; whisk together. Heat about 25 g (1 oz) butter in your omelette pan and when it's melted and frothy pour in the egg mixture. Just before the omelette is cooked to your liking – some people like them slightly runnier than I do – spread a quarter of the filling over the surface and fold it in half. Slip it on to a warmed plate and keep it in a cool oven while you make the rest.

Serve with warm brown rolls, and, if it is to be a supper dish, a green salad.

20 Scrambled Eggs with Smoked Salmon

This is a very ritzy and delicious way of serving scrambled eggs, and also an easy way of giving everyone a treat of a breakfast, lunch or quick supper. I like to fry small triangles of bread in a mixture of sunflower seed oil and butter, then drain them on kitchen paper, to serve with the scrambled eggs. These can be made ahead and kept warm for 2–3 hours.

Serves 6
12 large eggs
225 g (8 oz) smoked salmon, cut into 2.5 cm (1 in) strips
75 g (3 oz) butter
4 tbsp milk
salt and freshly ground black pepper
2–3 dashes hot pepper sauce (Tabasco)

Warm 6 serving plates.

Melt the butter in a large saucepan. Break the eggs into a bowl, add the milk, a little salt, lots of pepper and the hot pepper sauce; whisk well. Pour the eggs into the melted butter and, over a moderate heat, stir until they start to set. Take the saucepan off the heat while the eggs are still almost liquid, because they go on cooking off the heat.

Stir the strips of smoked salmon into the scrambled eggs, and leave for a minute to heat through. Divide the scrambled eggs between the plates, and arrange the triangles of fried bread around the edges. Serve at once because this, like all scrambled egg dishes, doesn't keep and is nicest eaten as soon as it is made.

21 Devilled Herring Roes on Toast

I don't particularly like the grainy-textured hard roes like cod's, but soft herring roes, devilled and served on buttered toast, is my idea of a perfect supper.

Serves 4
4 slices wholemeal bread, toasted and buttered
450 g (1 lb) soft herring roes
50 g (2 oz) butter
cayenne pepper
2 tsp Worcestershire sauce
4 lemon wedges to serve

Melt the butter in a frying pan and add the roes. Stir as they cook, and add the cayenne pepper – just a pinch unless you like very hot spicy tastes – and the Worcestershire sauce. Cook for about 5 minutes, then divide between the 4 slices of toast. Put a lemon wedge on the side of each plate and serve at once.

S·A·U·C·E·S F·O·R S·E·R·V·I·N·G
W·I·T·H F·I·S·H

—— COLD SAUCES ——
Mayonnaise
Tomato and Garlic Mayonnaise
Cucumber and Herb Mayonnaise
Curried Garlic Mayonnaise
Tartare Sauce
Tomato and Horseradish Cream

—— HOT SAUCES ——
Hollandaise
Fresh Tomato Sauce
Cream, Lemon and Chive Sauce
Mustard Sauce
Mushroom, Cheese and Cream Sauce
Betty Allen's Noilly Prat Sauce
Sauce Bercy
Horseradish and Parsley Sauce Messine

I am dividing this chapter into two sections, one for cold sauces, one for hot sauces. Some cold sauces are wonderful with hot dishes, for example, I like to serve Tomato and garlic mayonnaise with kebabs of bacon wrapped round scallops, or, traditionally, Tartare sauce is served with plain grilled fish. The Tomato sauce is a boon to calorie counters, and it freezes very well. Most of the other sauces are not to be recommended for those counting calories, but they are so delicious, and so fish-enhancing that they are worth it, and after all one doesn't eat a plateful of sauce, just a spoonful (or two).

COLD SAUCES

22 *Mayonnaise*

A good mayonnaise goes so well with prawns, or with dressed crab. I make mayonnaise of all kinds in either the liquidizer or the food processor, with half olive oil and half sunflower oil, as personally I find all olive oil too strong a flavour, apart from being very expensive. It keeps very well in a screw-topped jar in the fridge.

Makes about 275 ml (½ pt)
1 egg
1 egg yolk
1 rounded tsp dry mustard
1 tsp salt
about 12 grinds of pepper
1–1½ rounded tsp caster sugar
75 ml (3 fl oz) oil
2–3 tbsp wine vinegar

Put the egg, the yolk, mustard, salt, pepper and sugar into a liquidizer or food processor. Whiz, then very slowly add the oil, drip by drip. As the oil is used up you can add it in a steady trickle. Last, add the vinegar; taste after adding 2 tablespoons to see if it is sharp enough for your taste.

If things go wrong, which usually only happens if you are in a tremendous rush, don't despair. Tip the curdled mayonnaise into a jug, put an egg yolk into the liquidizer or processor, and whiz, very slowly adding the curdled mayonnaise, drop by drop, until it is all used up – the mayonnaise will be smooth and delicious, if slightly richer.

23 Tomato and Garlic Mayonnaise

One of my favourites, this can be served with virtually anything from cold prawns to barbecued salmon. It is also very good spread on wholemeal bread. It's best not to add the tomatoes more than the day before the sauce is to be eaten, because they tend to go mushy. The quantity of garlic added to this mayonnaise does depend on personal taste – my liking for it is almost an addiction, but too much masks the delicate flavour of the fish.

Serves 6
1 egg
1 egg yolk
1 rounded tsp dry mustard
1 tsp salt
about 12 grinds of black pepper
1½ tsp caster sugar
2 garlic cloves, skinned and chopped
150 ml (¼ pt) oil
2–3 tbsp wine vinegar
2 rounded tsp tomato purée
3 tomatoes, skinned, seeded and chopped

Put the egg, the yolk, mustard, salt, pepper, sugar and garlic into a liquidizer or food processor and whiz, then add the oil very slowly, drip by drip, until it is all used up. Still whizzing, add the vinegar and tomato purée. Pour the mayonnaise into a bowl, and stir in the chopped tomato flesh. Cover and keep in a cool place until ready to serve.

24 Cucumber and Herb Mayonnaise

This beautifully coloured, delicately flavoured mayonnaise with its pleasantly contrasting texture of chopped cucumber is perfect to serve with cold poached salmon. You can vary the herbs you put in according to what is available to you. It is delicious made with just parsley and chives, but even better if chervil and dill can be added too.

Serves 6
½ cucumber
1 egg
1 egg yolk
1 rounded tsp dry mustard
1 tsp salt
about 12 grinds of black pepper
1½ tsp sugar
about 150 ml (¼ pt) oil
2–3 tbsp wine vinegar
a handful of fresh parsley plus mint, chervil and dill

Start by preparing the cucumber. Peel it, cut in half lengthwise, scoop out the seeds, and cut the flesh into small dice. Sprinkle with some salt and leave for 30 minutes. Then drain the juices away and rinse the cucumber under running cold water. Pat dry with absorbent paper.

Put the egg, the yolk, mustard, salt, pepper and sugar into a liquidizer or food processor and whiz, then slowly add the oil, drop by drop. Then add the herbs – the blades of a processor will chop them, but if you are using a liquidizer it's easier to chop the herbs first. Lastly add the vinegar.

Pour the mayonnaise into a bowl and stir in the prepared cucumber. Cover and keep in the fridge until ready to serve.

25 Curried Garlic Mayonnaise

A most delicious mayonnaise, this is good to eat with any sort of fish or shellfish: hot, like scallop kebabs, or cold, like dressed crab. Served with some mushrooms, quickly cooked in a little hot oil and then cooled, and a few prawns, it makes a first course which always produces cries of delight from those eating it. The curry flavour should be very mild.

Serves 6
1 egg
1 egg yolk
1 rounded tsp dry mustard
1 tsp salt
2 garlic cloves, skinned and chopped
about 12 grinds of black pepper
2 tsp honey
2 tsp curry powder
about 275 ml (½ pt) oil
2–3 tbsp wine vinegar

Put the egg, the yolk, mustard, salt, garlic, pepper, honey and curry powder into a food processor or liquidizer, and whiz. Then slowly, drip by drip, add the oil, until it is all used up. Lastly add the vinegar. Pour into a bowl, cover and keep in the fridge until ready to serve.

26 Tartare Sauce

A classic sauce, this is so good I can eat it just spread on bread. But it is really meant to be served with fish or shellfish, either hot or cold.

Serves 6
2 egg yolks
½ tsp salt
about 12 grinds of black pepper
½ tsp sugar
150 ml (¼ pt) oil
2–3 tbsp wine vinegar
1 rounded tsp Dijon mustard
1 tsp chopped gherkins
1 tsp chopped capers
1 tbsp chopped parsley and chives
1 hard-boiled egg, finely chopped
6 black olives, stoned and chopped (optional)

Put the egg yolks into the liquidizer together with the salt, pepper and sugar and whiz. Gradually add the oil, drop by drop, until it is all used up. Then add the vinegar and mustard. Pour the mayonnaise into a bowl and stir the gherkins, capers, parsley and chives and lastly the hard-boiled egg. If you like, a few black olives can be added too.

27 Tomato and Horseradish Cream

This sauce makes a lighter alternative to mayonnaise-based sauces to eat with all sorts of cold fish or shellfish. The yoghurt helps to counteract the richness of shellfish, and it also goes well with cold fish and brown rice.

Serves 6
142 ml (¼ pt) double cream
2 × 142 g (5 oz) cartons natural yoghurt
2 heaped tsp plain horseradish (not horseradish sauce)
2 tbsp tomato ketchup
½ tsp salt
freshly ground black pepper
3 tomatoes, skinned, seeded and chopped

Whip the cream until fairly stiff. Fold in the yoghurt, horseradish, ketchup, seasoning and tomatoes. Cover and keep in the fridge until ready to serve.

HOT SAUCES

28 *Hollandaise*

I start this section with the classic sauce which seems synonymous with salmon when served hot: hollandaise. But hollandaise sauce is good with any fish. As well as with salmon, I serve it with salmon kedgeree. It will also 'dress up' the plainest piece of grilled fish and turn it into a luxury.

Some people find hollandaise easier to make in a liquidizer, but I find it so easily made in a bowl over a pan of simmering water that I can't think what the advantage is, and the liquidizer is just one more thing to wash up. Hollandaise sauce keeps hot over the hot water in the saucepan, on a gentle heat, with the odd whisk from time to time, but I wouldn't try to keep it for much more than 30 minutes. Should it show signs of separating, pour in a little boiling water and whisk vigorously, which usually does the trick and brings it back together again.

The precise flavour of hollandaise is a personal preference; I like mine quite sharp.

Serves 6
4 tbsp wine vinegar
1 bay leaf
1 blade of mace
1 slice of onion
a few peppercorns
3 egg yolks
175–200 g (6–7 oz) butter, cut into 6–7 pieces

Put the vinegar, bay leaf, mace, onion and peppercorns into a small saucepan and boil hard until the vinegar has reduced by about two-thirds. Strain. Break the yolks into a bowl, whisk in the vinegar, then put the bowl over a saucepan of very gently simmering water. Add a piece of the butter and stir (I use a wire whisk for this sauce) until it has melted and been incorporated into the yolk mixture. Add the butter, piece by piece, stirring, as the sauce thickens. Keep warm as described above.

If this sauce doesn't taste quite sharp enough for your liking, add some lemon juice. If it is a bit on the sharp side for you, add more butter.

29 Fresh Tomato Sauce

This is best made when there is a glut of tomatoes, and it freezes very well.
But it is also very good made with canned tomatoes. The sauce thickens as
it simmers, uncovered, and so it is a very good sauce for those of us who are
constantly watching our weight.

Serves 6
3 tbsp olive oil
1 onion, skinned and chopped
1 garlic clove, skinned and chopped
700 g (1½ lb) fresh tomatoes, quartered, or 2 × 425 g (15 oz) cans
   tomatoes
1 rounded tsp sugar
1 tsp salt
freshly ground black pepper
a small handful of fresh basil, or ½ tsp dried basil

Heat the olive oil in a saucepan and add the onion. Cook over a gentle heat,
stirring occasionally, for 5 minutes. Then add the garlic, tomatoes, sugar,
salt, plenty of pepper and the dried basil. (If you are using fresh basil wait
until the sauce is cooked before you add it.)

Let the sauce simmer, with the pan uncovered, for about 30–40
minutes, then draw the pan off the heat. Cool it a bit, add the fresh basil,
then liquidize and sieve the sauce; the tiny tomato pips don't break down in
the liquidizer. By sieving you get a velvet smooth sauce. Reheat to serve.

30 Cream, Lemon and Chive Sauce

It almost embarrasses me to include this sauce, it is so simple, but it is so good, especially with grilled trout or salmon, and I'm sure that by its very simplicity it will appeal to you as it does to me.

Serves 6
284 ml (½ pt) double cream
juice of 1 lemon
1 heaped tbsp finely chopped chives

Just put the cream into a saucepan, bring to the boil, then reduce the heat and stir in the lemon juice, but do not let the sauce boil again. Not long before serving stir in the chopped chives.

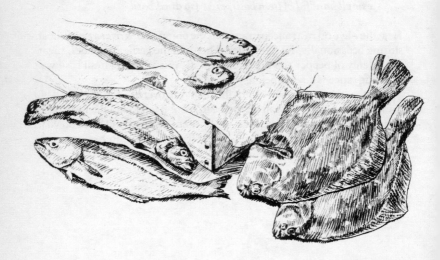

31 Mustard Sauce

Serve this sauce with herrings fried in oatmeal. I also like it with grilled mackerel.

Serves 6
50 g (2 oz) butter
1 onion, skinned and finely chopped
1 rounded tbsp flour
425 ml (¾ pt) milk
salt and freshly ground black pepper
1 generous tbsp French mustard

Melt the butter in a saucepan and add the onion. Cook over a gentle heat for about 5 minutes, until the onion is soft and transparent, then stir in the flour. Cook for a minute or two, then gradually add the milk, stirring all the time until the sauce boils. Season with a pinch of salt and pepper and the mustard.

Keep warm until ready to serve.

32 Mushroom, Cheese and Cream Sauce

An almost heavenly sauce for serving with any sort of fish or shellfish, it is extremely rich, so I suggest serving plain boiled brown rice and a green salad as accompaniments.

Serves 6
225 g (8 oz) button mushrooms, wiped and sliced
2–3 tbsp oil
175 g (6 oz) good Cheddar cheese, grated
284 ml (½ pt) double cream
juice of ½ lemon
pinch of thyme
pinch of salt and freshly ground pepper

Heat the oil in a frying pan and when it is very hot add the mushrooms – waiting till the oil is very hot will help prevent them shrinking. Cook for about half a minute, stirring, then transfer to a dish lined with absorbent paper to remove any excess moisture.

Put the other ingredients in a saucepan and heat gently, stirring until the cheese has melted into the cream. Stir in the cooked mushrooms and keep warm until you are ready to serve.

33 Betty Allen's Noilly Prat Sauce

This sauce is the perfect accompaniment to the Mousseline of scallops (rec. 61), but equally delicious with grilled sole, trout, or other shellfish.

Betty Allen, together with Eric, her husband, runs Airds Hotel in Port Appin, Argyll, renowned for its superb food, comfort and beautiful views.

Serves 6
4 tbsp Noilly Prat
¼ shallot, chopped (or 1 slice onion)
125 ml (4 fl oz) fish stock
142 ml (¼ pt) double cream
50 g (2 oz) butter, cut into 6 pieces
salt and freshly ground pepper

Put the shallot in a small saucepan together with the Noilly Prat and fish stock. Boil until the quantity is reduced by half. Then add the cream and boil again to reduce, until the sauce is the thickness of pouring cream. Strain and whisk the butter, a piece at a time, until the sauce is creamy. Season to taste. Pour over each mousseline.

34 Sauce Bercy

This is the way we make this classic sauce here at Kinloch, to serve with grilled trout or poached turbot. It is a sharp, refreshing sauce.

Serves 6
1 onion, skinned and finely chopped
4 tbsp dry white wine
50 ml (2 fl oz) fish stock
50 g (2 oz) butter, cut into 4 pieces
juice of ½ lemon
1 tbsp finely chopped parsley

Put the onion into a saucepan together with the wine and stock. Bring to the boil and simmer with the pan uncovered until the liquid has reduced by half. Whisk in the butter, a piece at a time. Whisk in the lemon juice, and just before serving (so it doesn't turn brown) stir in the parsley.

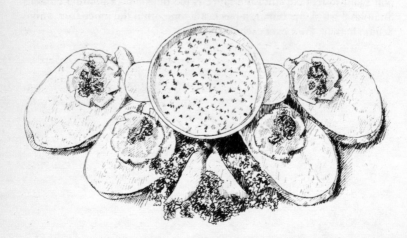

35 *Horseradish and Parsley Sauce Messine*

We serve this sauce with poached turbot or halibut. It is rather less rich than hollandaise, and the delicate flavours of the horseradish and parsley complement the fish perfectly.

Serves 6
284 ml (½ pt) single cream
50 g (2 oz) butter
1 tsp flour
2 egg yolks
1 tsp dry mustard
salt and freshly ground pepper
grated rind and juice of 1 lemon
2 rounded tsp horseradish
1 rounded tbsp finely chopped parsley

Put the cream, butter, flour, egg yolks, mustard, salt and pepper into a liquidizer or food processor and whiz until smooth. Pour into an ovenproof bowl and add the grated lemon rind. Put the bowl over a saucepan of simmering water, and stir from time to time until the sauce thickens to the consistency of fairly rich pouring cream. Mix in the lemon juice, horseradish and parsley.

Keep warm in the bowl over the pan of simmering water – the sauce won't curdle.

F·I·R·S·T C·O·U·R·S·E·S

Arbroath Smokie Pâté
Crab-stuffed Tomatoes
Crab with Tomato and Garlic Mayonnaise
Crab Ramekins au Gratin
Crab Crêpes
Mushroom and Prawn Cream Ramekins
Smoked Eel with Horseradish Cream
Gravad Lax
Smoked Haddock Roulade
Kipper Pâté
Anchovy Pâté
Lumpfish Caviar à la Crème
Kipper Mousse
Marinated Kipper Fillets
Prawn, Bacon and Cream Cheese Pâté
Grilled Oysters with Cream
Squid Fried in Olive Oil with Lemon Juice and Parsley
Squid Provençale
Prawn Cocktail
Pickled Herring and Apple Salad with Caraway Seeds
Potted Salmon with Orange and Walnuts
Taramasalata
Scallops Wrapped in Bacon and Grilled
Scallops Kinloch
Scallops Vinaigrette
Mousseline of Scallops
Potted Shrimps
Shrimp and Spinach Roulade
Shrimp Cheese Tartlets
Shrimp Mousse
Ceviche

Smoked Salmon Mousse
Smoked Trout and Horseradish Mousse
Sardine and Mushroom Pâté
Smoked Trout, Walnut and Cucumber Roulade
Mixed Seafood Mayonnaise
Fried Whitebait
Crab and Avocado Salad
Sweet and Sour Herrings
Shrimp Vol-Au-Vents
Prawn and Curry Cream Ramekins
Smoked Mackerel Pâté
Shrimps with Brown Bread and Walnut Rolls
Smoked Prawn Mayonnaise

36 Arbroath Smokie Pâté

Arbroath smokies are small haddock which have had their heads removed and been gutted, but been smoked just like that – as opposed to being flattened out like kippers. This pâté is one of the simplest, and one of the most delicious. As with all pâtés, it makes a superb filling for wholemeal rolls for picnics.

Serves 6
4 smokies (allow 6 if they are very small)
175 g (6 oz) butter
grated rind of 1 lemon
juice of 2 lemons
freshly ground black pepper
finely chopped parsley to garnish

Flake the flesh from the skins of the smokies, removing the bones at the same time. Put the flesh into a food processor or liquidizer.

Melt the butter over a low heat. Cool it a bit, then whiz the fish flesh in the food processor or liquidizer, slowly adding the butter, until it is all used up. Add the grated lemon rind and the juice, tasting as you do so, and don't add all the juice if you find the mixture is sufficiently lemony for your taste. Add plenty of pepper and scoop the pâté into a serving bowl or into individual ramekins.

Cover with cling film and put into the fridge until you are ready to serve. This pâté can be made 2–3 days ahead.

37 Crab-stuffed Tomatoes

When tomatoes are in abundance this makes an excellent first course, or part of a buffet lunch or supper. Serve with brown bread and butter.

Serves 6
12 medium tomatoes
450 g (1 lb) crabmeat, white and brown mixed
50 g (2 oz) long grain rice, cooked in chicken stock until tender,
*   drained, rinsed and cooled*
4 tbsp good mayonnaise
salt and freshly ground black pepper
finely chopped parsley

Start by preparing the tomatoes. You want them to stand on their stalk ends, so slice off about a quarter from the top of each one. With a pointed teaspoon or a knife and teaspoon, scoop out all the seeds from inside, trying not to split the skins. (Keep the tomato tops and seeds for making soup or tomato sauce.) Leave the empty tomatoes cut side down on a baking tray covered with absorbent paper.

Next mix together the crabmeat, cooked rice and mayonnaise, and season with pepper, and a little salt if you think it needs it. Put the tomatoes on a serving dish, and divide the crab mixture evenly between them. Sprinkle with finely chopped parsley and keep in the fridge until you are ready to serve them.

38 Crab with Tomato and Garlic Mayonnaise

This is one of my favourite ways of eating crab. It also seems to be very popular with our guests. I mix the white and brown crabmeats together, and serve 2 good spoonfuls (about 75 g (3 oz)) with Tomato and garlic mayonnaise (rec. 23) *beside* rather than over the crab. We serve this with our slightly malty, coarse brown bread.

39 Crab Ramekins au Gratin

This is how my husband Godfrey likes his crab, and it is a good way to serve crab hot in the winter months, when cold crab does not seem appropriate. As in all the crab recipes I mix the white and brown crabmeat together.

Serves 6
350 g (12 oz) crabmeat
50 g (2 oz) butter
1 rounded tbsp flour
275 ml (½ pt) milk
125 ml (4 fl oz) dry white wine
freshly grated nutmeg
salt and freshly ground black pepper
1 tsp English mustard
50 g (2 oz) good hard cheese, grated (I always use Lancashire)

Melt the butter in a saucepan, stir in the flour, let it cook for a minute, then gradually stir in the milk, followed by the white wine, stirring all the time until the sauce boils. Season with nutmeg, salt and pepper to taste and the mustard. (If you don't have ready-made mustard, only powder, add it with the flour.) Heat the grill.

Stir the crabmeat into the sauce and divide the mixture between 6 ramekins. Sprinkle the cheese over each ramekin and grill to melt and brown the cheese before serving.

40 Crab Crêpes

Pancakes filled with crab in a creamy sauce with just a hint of curry in it make a sumptuous first course, but they are also an ideal lunch or supper dish, as they are fairly filling. As a main course, I serve them with a green salad and warm brown rolls. They freeze very well.

Serves 6 as a first course, 4 as a main course
125 g (4 oz) plain flour
1 egg
1 egg yolk
275 ml (½ pt) milk
1 tbsp oil
butter for frying
For the filling
350 g (12 oz) crabmeat, white and brown mixed
50 g (2 oz) butter
50 g (2 oz) flour
575 ml (1 pt) milk
125 g (4 oz) Lancashire or other hard cheese, grated
salt and freshly ground black pepper
freshly grated nutmeg
¼ tsp curry powder

Mix all the batter ingredients except the butter in a liquidizer, whiz until smooth, and leave for 30 minutes before making up the pancakes.

In a small frying pan, ideally about 15 cm (6 in) across, heat a small nut of butter, then pour in a small amount of pancake batter. Swirl it round the pan so that it forms a thin film over the base – it should be as thin as possible. I use a small palette knife and my fingers to turn the pancake over to cook on its other side. Keep the pancakes on a wire rack as they are made. Allow 2 per person for a first course, 3 if it is to be a main course.

To make the filling melt the butter and stir in the flour. Cook for a minute or two, then gradually add the milk, stirring all the time until the sauce boils. Season with salt, pepper, nutmeg and curry powder, then stir in nearly all the grated cheese – leave a little for sprinkling over the filled pancakes. Stir the crabmeat into the sauce, and divide it evenly between the pancakes, rolling each into a fat roll. Place them side by side in a buttered ovenproof dish and sprinkle with the remaining cheese. You can prepare the dish up to this stage in the morning.

Before serving, heat in a moderate oven (180°C, 350°F, gas 4) for about 25 minutes, until the crêpes are heated through and the cheese has melted on the top.

41 Mushroom and Prawn Cream Ramekins

This is a very rich first course, but oh so good. It would be best to follow it with a fairly plain and simple main course – perhaps a plain roast or grilled fish with a tomato sauce.

Serves 6
225 g (8 oz) button mushrooms, wiped and sliced
1 tbsp oil
25 g (1 oz) butter
squeeze of lemon juice
pinch of dried thyme or a sprig of fresh thyme
200 g (7 oz) good Cheddar cheese, grated
284 ml (½ pt) double cream
salt and freshly ground pepper
175 g (6 oz) shelled prawns
50 g (2 oz) breadcrumbs

Put the butter and oil together in a frying pan. When the butter is melted and oil very hot, add the mushrooms and cook very fast for a minute or two, turning the slices. Remove to a dish, squeeze lemon juice over them and sprinkle with the thyme.

Put the cream and 175 g (6 oz) of the cheese in a saucepan and cook over a gentle heat until the cheese has melted. Season with salt and pepper to taste. Drain any juice off the cooked mushrooms and stir them into the cheesy cream together with the prawns. Divide this heavenly mixture between 6 ramekins.

Mix the breadcrumbs and remaining cheese together and sprinkle a little on top of each ramekin. Before serving put the ramekins under a hot grill to melt the cheese and toast the crumbs.

42 Smoked Eel with Horseradish Cream

A lot of people think that smoked eel is by far the greatest delicacy of all the smoked fish. Really good smoked eel is rich and succulent, and I love it with this horseradish cream. It is a very convenient first course, because the cream can be made up 2 days ahead, and kept in the fridge until you are ready to arrange the smoked eel on the serving plates. The parsley in the cream sauce is optional, but I think that it gives a fresh flavour to the cream, and makes it look more attractive.

Serves 6
225 g (8 oz) smoked eel, sliced
284 ml (½ pt) double cream, whipped
1–2 tbsp lemon juice
1 tbsp dried horseradish
1 tbsp finely chopped parsley (optional)

Mix all the above ingredients together, and serve in generous spoonfuls at the side of the smoked eel on each plate. Accompany it with brown bread and butter.

Note: dried horseradish can be found in good grocers' and delicatessen shops. It has a better flavour than horseradish sauce, which is very vinegary.

43 Gravad Lax

Many people prefer gravad lax to smoked salmon. Both are great delicacies. Gravad lax is salmon preserved with dill, sugar and white pepper. It is sliced just like smoked salmon, and is very easy to prepare yourself. Although this is much better made with fresh dill you can use dried if fresh is not available.

For a 1 kilo (2 lb) piece of salmon
2 tbsp salt
2 tbsp sugar
2 tsp freshly ground white pepper
lots of dill leaves

Bone and fillet the fish but leave the skin on. Put a thick layer of dill on the bottom of a shallow dish. Mix together the salt, sugar and pepper and rub half this mixture into the flesh side of one piece of fish. Put this skin down on the dill. Rub the remaining mixture into the other piece of fish. Cover the first piece with a thick layer of dill and put the second piece of fish on top, skin side uppermost. Cover with cling film and weight it down with a board and some heavy cans on top.

Turn the fish over each day and leave for 3–4 days. Slice thinly to serve.

44 Smoked Haddock Roulade

This can be a first course or a very good lunch or supper dish. For a special occasion it can be filled with scallops in a creamy sauce.

Serves 8
700 g (1½ lb) smoked haddock
0.8 litre (1½ pt) milk and water mixed
1 onion, skinned
1 blade of mace
50 g (2 oz) butter
50 g (2 oz) plain flour
pinch of freshly grated nutmeg
freshly ground black pepper
4 eggs, separated
50 g (2 oz) Cheddar cheese, grated
For the filling
6 hard-boiled eggs
50 g (2 oz) butter
40 g (1½ oz) plain flour
575 ml (1 pt) milk
75 g (3 oz) Cheddar cheese, grated
pinch of freshly ground nutmeg
1 tsp English mustard
salt and freshly ground black pepper

Put the fish, milk and water in a saucepan together with the onion and mace and bring slowly to the boil. Simmer very gently for 5 minutes, then remove from the heat and leave for 10 minutes. Strain off the cooking liquid and keep it – it's so easy to throw it out in an absent-minded moment. You need it to make the roulade. Flake the fish from the skin, removing the bones.

Line a 30 × 35 cm (12 × 14 in) Swiss roll tin with a piece of baking paper (siliconized greaseproof paper).

Melt the butter in a saucepan. Add the flour and cook over a gentle heat for a couple of minutes. Then gradually add just over 575 ml (1 pt) of the liquid the fish cooked in, stirring all the time until the sauce boils. Take the saucepan off the heat, season with nutmeg and pepper to taste, and cool for 10–15 minutes. Then beat in the 4 egg yolks and stir in the prepared fish.

Lastly whisk the egg whites until very stiff, and, using a metal spoon, quickly and thoroughly fold them into the fish sauce mixture. Sprinkle a little of the grated cheese on the siliconized paper and pour the smoked haddock mixture over it, smoothing it evenly, and bake in a moderate oven (180°C, 350°F, gas 4) for 20–30 minutes, until it feels firm to the touch.

Meanwhile make the filling. Melt the butter in a saucepan and stir in the flour. Cook for a couple of minutes, then gradually add the milk, stirring all the time until the sauce boils. Stir in the cheese, nutmeg, mustard, a little salt and pepper. Remove the pan from the heat. Chop the hard-boiled eggs and stir them into the sauce.

When the roulade is cooked, take it out of the oven. Put a fresh piece of siliconized paper on the work surface. Take a short side of the paper containing the roulade in each hand and turn it on to the clean piece. Carefully peel the old paper off the roulade. Cover the surface with the cheesy egg sauce and roll the roulade up from one long side. Ease the roulade on to a serving dish, sprinkle with a little more grated cheese and serve within 20 minutes.

45 Kipper Pâté

Recipes go in and out of fashion just like clothes, and this is one which seems to be *out*, having been very much *in* about 10 years ago. It is a great pity because it is very easy, can be made 3–4 days in advance and, most important of all, is delicious. It also makes an excellent filling for soft brown rolls for picnics.

Serves 6
3 large juicy kippers
juice of 2 lemons
100 g (3½ oz) butter, melted over a low heat
freshly ground black pepper
1 heaped tbsp finely chopped parsley

Poach the kippers in a frying pan half full of water for 7–10 minutes. Turn the kippers over as they cook. Remove from the water on to a dish covered with absorbent paper and cool. Then flake the flesh from the bones and skin, picking out as many of the bones as you can. Put the flesh into a food processor, if you have one, or in small amounts into a liquidizer. Blend and whiz the kipper flesh, adding the butter slowly until it is all used up. Then slowly add the lemon juice, tasting as you go to see it is not too sharp for your liking. Season with plenty of pepper, and the parsley.

Scoop the pâté into a serving dish or individual ramekins, cover with cling film and keep in the fridge until you are ready to serve it.

46 Anchovy Pâté

This recipe was given to me by Char Donaldson, who is a good friend of ours and an extremely good cook. It is very rich, but divine for those who love anchovies. Like the kipper pâté it is a good filling for brown rolls, together with sliced tomatoes.

Serves 4–6
225 g (8 oz) packet Philadelphia cream cheese
50 g (2 oz) can anchovies, drained
100 g (3½ oz) butter

Put all the above ingredients in a food processor or liquidizer and whiz until smooth.

47 *Lumpfish Caviar à la Crème*

This is an invaluable recipe because it takes seconds to prepare and is very dinner-party worthy. You can also use it as a filling for cheese profiteroles. Serve with brown bread and butter.

Serves 6
50 g (2 oz) jar Danish lumpfish roe
juice of 1 lemon
284 ml (½ pt) double cream
chopped chives to garnish

Whip the cream, incorporating the lemon juice. Stir in the lumpfish roe and divide between 6 small ramekins. Sprinkle a few chopped chives on each one just before serving. It will keep in the fridge for 24 hours, covered with cling film.

48 *Kipper Mousse*

This creamy, tasty mousse makes a successful first course for a dinner party. It can be made 2 days in advance and kept, covered with cling film, in the fridge.

Serves 6–8
*3 large kippers, cooked, with the flesh flaked from the skin and as
    many of the bones removed as possible*
*1 envelope gelatine powder, dissolved in 150 ml (¼ pt) water over a
    low heat*
284 ml (½ pt) double cream
4–5 tbsp lemon juice
freshly ground black pepper
2 egg whites
finely chopped parsley to garnish

Put the kipper flesh into a food processor or liquidizer, and whiz, pouring in the dissolved gelatine and half the cream. Whip the remaining cream. Whiz in the lemon juice, then scoop the mixture out into a bowl, fold in the whipped cream and season with plenty of pepper. Lastly whisk the egg whites until very stiff, and fold them into the kipper mixture.

Pour into a serving dish, or into individual ramekins if you prefer. Serve sprinkled with finely chopped parsley, accompanied by brown bread and butter.

49 Marinated Kipper Fillets

Anyone who, like me, loves smoked fish will love this. It has the added bonus of being very easy to put together, and benefits from being made at least 24 hours ahead of being eaten.

Serves 6
6 kipper fillets
1 small onion, skinned and thinly sliced
1 rounded tsp caster sugar
1 rounded tsp mustard powder
3 tbsp white wine vinegar
4 tbsp olive or sunflower oil
freshly ground black pepper

Skin the fillets, using a very sharp knife – this doesn't take a second. Cut each fillet in half lengthwise, and put the pieces on a shallow dish. Cover evenly with the slices of onion.

Mix the remaining ingredients together and pour over the fillets. Leave for at least 24 hours. Drain off the marinade and serve the kipper fillets with brown bread and butter. If the weather is hot keep the dish, covered with cling film, in the fridge. If it isn't too hot it can be kept in a cool place.

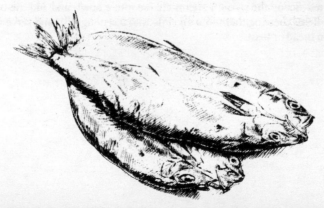

50 Prawn, Bacon and Cream Cheese Pâté

Bacon goes well with fish and shellfish in particular. This pâté is very easy and quick to make, and heavenly to eat. The only fiddly bit is shelling the prawns, but it's worth every minute.

Serves 6
75 g (3 oz) cooked, shelled prawns
3 rashers smoked bacon
225 g (8 oz) cream cheese
1 garlic clove, skinned and finely chopped
1 tbsp lemon juice
freshly ground black pepper
1 rounded tbsp finely chopped parsley

Chop the prawns. Dry fry the bacon until crisp, drain on absorbent paper and break it into small pieces. If you have a food processor put the cream cheese into it and whiz until smooth. Otherwise put it into a sturdy bowl and pound it until it is as smooth as possible.

Don't add the rest of the ingredients to the food processor, because the whole pâté will become too smooth; one of its attractions is the different textures. Scoop the smooth cream cheese into a bowl, and add the other ingredients, beating them in well. Pile into a serving dish and serve with brown bread or toast.

51 Grilled Oysters with Cream

I think oysters are one of those things you either love or loathe. Personally, I loathe them unless they are cooked, when I love them. This is a very easy, very luxurious recipe; the number of oysters you allow per person is up to you. But I would suggest 6 per person is quite generous served this way.

Serves 2
12 oysters on the half shell
125 ml (4 fl oz) double cream
freshly ground black pepper
1–2 tbsp grated Parmesan cheese

Heat the grill. Take each oyster off its shell. Put a spoonful of cream into each shell and grind some black pepper on top. Put the oysters back and sprinkle each one with a little Parmesan cheese. Put the shells on to a baking tray and grill for about 3 minutes. Serve with brown bread and butter.

52 Squid Fried in Olive Oil with Lemon Juice and Parsley

Squid is so good I love it however it's cooked. This is the simplest of ways and one of the best. I find squid is very filling, so don't be too generous.

Serves 6
450 g (1 lb) prepared squid, flesh and tentacles cut in rings
6 tbsp olive oil
salt and freshly ground black pepper
1 tbsp very finely chopped parsley
1 garlic clove, skinned and very finely chopped
6 lemon wedges

Put the olive oil in a frying pan and heat until very hot. Add the prepared squid and cook, stirring all the time, for 3–5 minutes *only*. Add the garlic while the squid is cooking, with a little salt and plenty of pepper. Stir in the parsley just before the cooking time is up. Serve hot with a large lemon wedge on each plate.

53 *Squid Provençale*

The classic Provençale combination of garlic, tomato and basil makes the perfect sauce for squid. In more generous quantities this makes a very good main course for lunch or supper.

Serves 6
450 g (1 lb) prepared squid, chopped in rings and with the tentacles
    in about 5 cm (2 in) pieces
6 tbsp olive oil
1 large onion, skinned and finely chopped
1 large garlic clove, skinned and finely chopped
425 g (15 oz) can tomatoes
½ tsp sugar
salt and freshly ground black pepper
a few sprigs of fresh basil, roughly chopped; or ½ tsp dried basil
finely chopped parsley (optional)

Put half the olive oil into a saucepan and heat, then add the onion and cook gently for about 5 minutes, until it is soft and transparent. Then add the garlic and cook a further couple of minutes. Pour in the tomatoes, crushing them against the sides of the pan with the back of the wooden spoon to break them up. Stir in the sugar, salt to taste, plenty of pepper and the basil. Leave the sauce to simmer, uncovered, for 30–40 minutes until it is thick.

You can make the sauce in the morning for dinner that night, or up to 2 days ahead and keep it in the fridge, covered with cling film.

Heat the remaining olive oil in a frying pan and add the squid. Cook for about 5 minutes, stirring occasionally to make sure they cook all over. Stir the squid into the tomato sauce (reheat if made ahead) and serve sprinkled with parsley, with brown bread to mop up the juices.

This is also very good served cold, on a hot summer's day, sprinkled with chopped fresh basil leaves.

54 Prawn Cocktail

Prawn cocktail is found on menus all over the world. It can be nasty and mean – a restaurateur's cheat dish, with a very few prawns hidden in lots of lettuce, their flavour drowned in beastly vinegary sauce. It is such a shame, because a properly made prawn cocktail provides a rich and creamy first course, with the sharpness coming not from vinegar but from lemon. If you can get fresh prawns they are much tastier than frozen, but frozen are much better than canned. I believe in being generous with the prawns, and making a really filling first course.

Serves 6
450 g (1 lb) shelled cooked prawns – if they are very large cut them in half
284 ml (½ pt) double cream
1 tbsp tomato purée
2–3 tbsp lemon juice, to taste
1 tbsp Worcestershire sauce
½ garlic clove, skinned and crushed with salt
freshly ground black pepper
1 iceberg or other crisp lettuce, washed and dried
finely chopped parsley to garnish

Whip the cream with the tomato purée, lemon juice, Worcestershire sauce, garlic and plenty of pepper. This can be done in advance and kept in a covered bowl until you are ready to assemble the cocktails in the evening. Just before serving, shred the lettuce finely and put enough in each glass or dish to fill it about one-third full. Stir the prawns into the cream and divide evenly between the serving dishes. Sprinkle with finely chopped parsley. Serve with brown bread and butter.

55 Pickled Herring and Apple Salad with Caraway Seeds

For those who love pickled herrings, like my husband who will eat them at any time of the day or night, this first course is a favourite. It also makes a lovely salad in the summer, eaten as a main course.

Serves 6
6 pickled herrings
3 apples, preferably Cox's
142 ml (¼ pt) soured cream
1 tsp caraway seeds
finely chopped parsley
freshly ground black pepper
iceberg or other crisp lettuce, washed and dried

Unroll the herrings and remove any sliced onions rolled up inside them. Cut the herrings into 2.5 cm (1 in) chunks.

Quarter and core the apples, but leave their skins on. Cut them into little chunks, about 1 cm (½ in) in size.

Stir the cream, caraway seeds, parsley and pepper together. Stir the herring and apple pieces into the cream mixture.

Arrange some shredded lettuce on serving plates and divide the herring mixture between them. Serve with warm rolls and butter.

56 Potted Salmon with Orange and Walnuts

This is a good way of using up left-over salmon and turning it into a sophisticated first course. The combination of orange and walnuts goes well with salmon, and the crunchiness of the walnuts contrasts with the smooth texture of the pâté.

Serves 6
150 g (5 oz) butter
½ tsp salt
75 g (3 oz) walnuts, broken into bits
350 g (12 oz) cooked salmon, skinned and flaked from the bones
grated rind of 1 large or 2 small oranges
juice of 1 lemon
freshly ground black pepper
pinch of freshly grated nutmeg

Melt the butter in a saucepan. Pour most of it into a bowl or jug to cool, leaving about 2 tablespoons in the pan. Add the salt and walnuts and fry over a moderate heat for about 5 minutes, stirring from time to time. Tip them on to a double thickness of absorbent paper to cool.

Put the flaked salmon into a food processor. (You can do this in a liquidizer but it is quite hard work as you have to keep stopping and pushing the salmon down on to the blades.) Add the grated orange rind and whiz. Then add the lemon juice and whiz again. Slowly add the cooled, melted butter, until it is all blended into the salmon purée. Season with plenty of pepper and the nutmeg. Stir in the prepared walnuts – don't whiz them in, or the pâté will lose its contrasting textures.

Put the salmon mixture into a serving dish and serve with brown bread or toast.

57 *Taramasalata*

Chocolate cake, good vanilla ice-cream and homemade taramasalata rate very high on my list of personal addictions. There are so many variations, but it is basically a cod's roe pâté. Never having been to Greece, the country of its origin, I don't really know how authentic my version is, but I love it so much I am quite capable of eating a whole batch on my own.

Serves 6
*225 g (8 oz) smoked cod's roe, scraped from its skin; or use a 225 g
   (8 oz) jar
2 garlic cloves, skinned
3 slices white bread, crusts cut off, soaked in cold water to cover
juice of 2 lemons
200 ml (7 fl oz) olive oil
freshly ground black pepper
toast and black olives to serve*

Put the smoked cod's roe into a food processor or liquidizer. Squeeze the bread free of water and add it to the fish with the garlic. Whiz, slowly adding the lemon juice. Then slowly add the olive oil, whizzing all the time. If the mixture is very stiff, add a couple of tablespoons of cold water. It should be the consistency of fairly stiffly whipped cream. Whiz in plenty of pepper, then scoop the pâté into a serving dish. Serve with hot toast and lots of black olives.

Delicious Fish

58 Scallops Wrapped in Bacon and Grilled

Bacon and shellfish again – this time the bacon is wrapped around the scallops to keep them juicy as they cook. This is so simple, yet so good. If the bacon and scallop rolls are pushed on to skewers, they barbecue beautifully. I like to serve them with Tomato and garlic mayonnaise (rec. 23).

Serves 6
18 large scallops, cut in half
18 streaky bacon rashers, cut in half
oil for brushing

Heat the grill. Wrap a piece of bacon around each halved scallop and push on to a skewer (allow 1 skewer per person). Alternatively, fasten each roll with a wooden toothpick. Brush each roll with a little oil and grill, turning them so they cook on all sides, until the bacon is sizzling and crisp.

If you barbecue them they take about 20 minutes; turn the skewers to make sure they cook evenly.

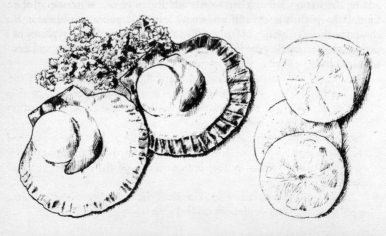

59 *Scallops Kinloch*

The scallops in this recipe are cooked in a delicately flavoured sauce with just a hint of curry.

Serves 6
18 large scallops
1 tbsp desiccated coconut
1.1 litres (2 pt) milk and water mixed
a few black peppercorns
1 onion, skinned and roughly chopped
25 g (1 oz) butter
1 small onion, skinned and very finely chopped
25 g (1 oz) flour
1 tsp curry powder
2 tsp tomato purée
juice of 1 lemon
salt and freshly ground black pepper
parsley to garnish

Pour 150 ml (¼ pt) of boiling water on to the coconut and leave to soak for 10 minutes. Put the scallops in a pan with the milk and water, peppercorns and onion. Place on a moderate heat and bring to simmering point; simmer very gently for 5 minutes. Take the pan off the heat and leave the scallops to cool in the liquid for about 15 minutes.

Melt the butter in another saucepan, add the finely chopped onion and cook for about 5 minutes, until the onion is soft and transparent, stirring occasionally. Mix in the flour and curry powder and cook for a further couple of minutes.

Strain the liquid the scallops cooked in into a measuring jug and gradually add about 575 ml (1 pt) to the sauce, stirring all the time until it boils. Stir in the tomato purée, lemon juice and the strained coconut water. Season to taste.

Cut the scallops into large chunks and stir them into the sauce. Serve on heated serving dishes or plates sprinkled with finely chopped parsley.

60 *Scallops* Vinaigrette

This is a lovely way to serve scallops: the vinaigrette dressing is poured on to them while they are still hot so that they absorb its flavour. I like to serve them with garlic rolls – brown rolls split and spread generously with garlic butter, then wrapped in foil and warmed in the oven until the butter has melted. Scallops vinaigrette can be eaten hot or cold, but I prefer them cold.

Serves 6
18 large scallops
0.8 litre (1½ pt) water
275 ml (½ pt) dry white wine
a few peppercorns
1 onion, skinned and quartered
For the sauce
½ tsp salt
½ tsp caster sugar
1 tsp freshly ground black pepper
1 tsp mustard powder
1 tbsp finely chopped parsley
1 tbsp lemon juice
1 tbsp white wine vinegar
5 tbsp olive oil

Put the scallops into a saucepan with the water, wine, peppercorns and onion. Place on a moderate heat and bring to simmering point. Simmer gently for 5 minutes, then remove the pan from the heat and leave the scallops in the liquid for 10 minutes.

Meanwhile make the sauce: whiz all the sauce ingredients in a liquidizer. Remove the scallops from the liquid and cut them into large chunks – about 3 pieces from each. Pour the sauce on to the hot scallops and stir it through them. Leave until cold to serve.

61 Mousseline of Scallops

This recipe comes from Betty Allen, a great friend of ours who, together with her husband Eric, runs one of the best hotels in Scotland, Airds Hote¹ at Port Appin. This is an exquisite dish. Its sauce is to be found in the chapter on sauces. This fills 6 small ramekins.

Serves 6
6 large scallops – approx. 175 g (6 oz)
80 g (3¼ oz) whiting, sole, or halibut
a pinch of salt, freshly ground pepper
a pinch of cayenne
275 ml (½ pt) double cream

Dry the scallops on kitchen paper. Put them into a food processor (or mince them finely) together with the whiting (sole or halibut). Scrape into a bowl, and put the bowl over a basin full of ice. Season the fish purée with salt, pepper and cayenne. Press the mixture through a sieve, and keep cold. Add the double cream and sieve again. Divide the mixture between the ramekins and tap to get rid of air. Poach in a bain-marie for about 20 minutes, in a moderate oven (180°C, 350°F, gas 4). Allow to rest for 4–5 minutes before serving, so that the mousseline comes away from the mould or ramekin. Cover with the Noilly Prat sauce, and serve immediately.

62 *Potted Shrimps*

I come from Lancashire, and Morecambe Bay is about half an hour's drive from my parents' home, where the best shrimps in the world are found. Tiny and pink, with a faintly peppery taste, they are good served just plain with lemon juice squeezed over them, and with brown bread and butter as an accompaniment. I do admire the people who gather them, and also those who painstakingly shell these tiny shrimps, as so far there has been no mechanical invention to do the job. Potted shrimps are a great treat, and very convenient, as they can be prepared the day before and left, covered, in the fridge until required.

Serves 6
450 g (1 lb) shrimps
225 g (8 oz) butter
½ tsp ground mace
freshly ground black pepper
6 lemon wedges to serve

Put the shrimps in a bowl. Put the butter in a saucepan to melt over a low heat. Pour about three-quarters of the melted butter into the bowl of shrimps. Add the mace and black pepper, and stir and fold all together thoroughly.

Divide evenly between 6 ramekin dishes, pour a little of the remaining butter over each ramekin. Cover and keep in the fridge.

Serve with a large lemon wedge with each ramekin and a plate of brown bread and butter.

63 Shrimp and Spinach Roulade

This is a lovely way of serving shrimps hot, and it makes a very special first course. It can also be a substantial main course for lunch or supper, to feed 4–6 people.

Serves 6–8
450 g (1 lb) shrimps
25 g (1 oz) butter
25 g (1 oz) flour
275–425 ml (½–¾ pt) milk
pinch of freshly grated nutmeg
salt and freshly ground black pepper
For the roulade
900 g (2 lb) frozen spinach, thawed and drained of all its water
25 g (1 oz) butter
4 eggs, separated
salt and freshly ground black pepper
pinch of freshly grated nutmeg

Line a Swiss roll tin about 25 × 30 cm (10 × 12 in) with a piece of baking paper (siliconized greaseproof paper).

First make the roulade. Put the prepared spinach into a food processor and whiz, adding the butter and the egg yolks, one by one, and seasoning with salt, pepper and nutmeg. If you don't have a food processor, chop the spinach first and use a liquidizer.

Whisk the egg whites until they are very stiff and, using a metal spoon, fold them into the spinach purée quickly but thoroughly. Pour into the lined tin, smooth it even, and bake in a moderate oven (180°C, 350°F, gas 4) for 20–25 minutes, until firm to the touch.

While the roulade is cooking make the shrimp sauce. Melt the butter, stir in the flour, and cook for a minute or two, then, stirring, gradually add enough milk to make a thick sauce. Season with nutmeg, salt and pepper. Stir until the sauce boils, then take the pan off the heat and mix in the shrimps.

When the roulade is cooked, remove it from the oven. Put a fresh piece of baking paper on a work surface and tip the cooked mixture on to it.

Carefully peel the old paper off the back of the spinach mixture. Spread the shrimp sauce all over the surface and roll up lengthwise, easing the roulade on to a serving dish, like a long Swiss roll.

Cut in thick slices to serve. Try not to keep it for much more than 15 minutes before serving.

64 Shrimp Cheese Tartlets

These extravagant cheese pastry tartlets with their shrimp sauce filling are divine, and worth every minute of the time it takes to make them, which isn't much anyway. They are rather filling, so if you plan to serve them as a first course, have a simple main course and light dessert to follow.

Serves 6
For the pastry
175 g (6 oz) butter, hard from the fridge
175 g (6 oz) plain flour
175 g (6 oz) Cheddar cheese, grated
1 egg yolk
1 rounded tsp dry mustard
For the sauce
450 g (1 lb) shrimps
25 g (1 oz) butter
25 g (1 oz) flour
about 425 ml (¾ pt) milk
salt and freshly ground black pepper
freshly grated nutmeg
parsley or paprika to garnish

If you have a food processor, whiz all the pastry ingredients together until they form a solid ball. If you haven't, rub the butter into the flour until it is crumb-like, then rub in the grated cheese and mustard, and work in the egg yolk. Rest it in the fridge before rolling out.

Divide the pastry into 2 and roll out the first bit on a floured work surface. Use it to line 3 tartlet tins, about 10 cm (4 in) across, and then roll out the other piece of pastry and line the remaining 3 tins. Put the pastry-lined tins in the fridge for at least 30 minutes. (Any left-over scraps of pastry can be rolled out and cut with a small pastry cutter into round biscuits about 4 cm (1½ in) across, baked in a moderate oven and kept in an airtight tin to serve with drinks – but not on the same evening as you plan to serve the tartlets.)

Put the tartlets on a baking sheet and bake in a moderate oven (180°C, 350°F, gas 4) for 20–25 minutes, until the pastry is just beginning to shrink away from the sides of the tins. Leave to cool.

Meanwhile make the sauce. Melt the butter in a saucepan and stir in the flour. Cook for a minute or two, then gradually stir in the milk. Stir continuously until the sauce boils, then remove from the heat. Season with salt, pepper and nutmeg to taste and stir in the shrimps.

You can make the pastry tartlets in the morning for dinner that evening, or even the previous day. Before you reheat them, ease the pastry cases out of their tins and on to small heatproof serving plates. This is much easier to do when the pastry is cold. Put the plates into a low oven to warm the pastry through. Just before your guests sit down divide the hot shrimp sauce between the cheese tartlets, and dust each one with finely chopped parsley or a little paprika.

65 Shrimp Mousse

I like to reserve some shrimps to scatter in a circle round the edge of the mousse, or mousses if I serve it in ramekins.

Serves 6
450 g (1 lb) shrimps
200 ml (7 fl oz) milk
3 large eggs, separated
1 scant tsp cornflour
2 tbsp water
2 tsp gelatine
142 ml (¼ pt) soured cream (or double cream soured with lemon juice)
salt and freshly ground black pepper
freshly grated nutmeg

Heat the milk in a saucepan. Beat the yolks together with the cornflour, pour on a little of the hot milk, then pour the yolk mixture into the milk and cook over a gentle heat, stirring all the time, until the sauce is thick enough to coat the back of the wooden spoon. Sprinkle the gelatine on to the water, let it soak for a minute or two, then add this to the hot sauce, stirring until it is dissolved. Sieve the sauce to strain off any stringy bits of yolk and leave to cool. When it is quite cold stir in the soured cream and salt, pepper and nutmeg to taste.

Reserve about a quarter of the shrimps for garnishing; put the remainder into a food processor or liquidizer and whiz into a purée. Fold this into the cold creamy mixture. Lastly whisk the egg whites until very stiff and, using a metal spoon, fold them quickly but thoroughly into the shrimp mixture.

Pour and scoop the mousse into a serving bowl, or into ramekins if you prefer. Arrange the reserved shrimps round the edges of the mousse, or, if they are in ramekins, make a small heap in the middle of each. Serve with brown bread and butter.

66 *Ceviche*

I generally use turbot to make ceviche, but any firm white fish is suitable. The acid lemon juice and vinegar marinade softens the fish without it being cooked. I like to serve the small cubes of fish with Tomato and garlic mayonnaise (rec. 23).

Serves 6
700 g (1½ lb) turbot, cut into 1 cm (½ in) cubes or strips
150 ml (¼ pt) lemon juice
150 ml (¼ pt) white wine vinegar

Put the fish into a shallow dish and pour the lemon juice and vinegar mixture over. Leave it for at least 3 hours – I get it ready in the morning for dinner that evening.

Drain off the marinade and serve the fish with a large spoonful of Tomato and garlic mayonnaise beside it.

67 Smoked Salmon Mousse

We are very lucky in having a salmon-processing factory in Inverness where very good offcuts of smoked salmon can be bought at very reasonable prices. Similar trimmings can sometimes be found in fishmongers, and they are ideal for making this smooth-textured creamy first course.

Serves 6
275 g (10 oz) smoked salmon
½ chicken stock cube
2 tsp gelatine
142 ml (¼ pt) single cream
2 tbsp lemon juice
freshly ground black pepper
freshly grated nutmeg
284 ml (½ pt) double cream, whipped
2 egg whites
parsley and/or lemon slices to garnish (optional)

Sprinkle the stock cube and gelatine over 4 tablespoons of water and place over a very low heat to dissolve.

Put the smoked salmon into a food processor or liquidizer and whiz, adding the single cream, lemon juice, plenty of pepper and a pinch of nutmeg. Add the dissolved gelatine and scoop the mixture into a bowl. Fold in the whipped cream. Lastly whisk the egg whites until they are very stiff and, using a metal spoon, fold them quickly but thoroughly into the smoked salmon mixture. Divide between 6 large ramekins and leave to set. Sprinkle finely chopped parsley over the surface of each before serving, if you like, or garnish with a thin slice of lemon or both.

68 Smoked Trout and Horseradish Mousse

Rich, succulent smoked trout is now quite widely available, and the sharp flavour of horseradish complements it perfectly.

Serves 6
2 smoked trout, flesh flaked from the bones
2 tsp gelatine
142 ml (¼ pt) single cream
2 tsp dried horseradish
3 tbsp lemon juice
freshly ground black pepper
284 ml (½ pt) double cream, whipped
2 egg whites
chopped parsley or lemon slices to garnish (optional)

Sprinkle the gelatine over 4 tablespoons of water and place over a very low heat to dissolve.

Put the fish into a food processor or liquidizer and whiz, adding the single cream, lemon juice, horseradish and plenty of pepper. Add the dissolved gelatine and scoop the mixture into a bowl. Fold in the whipped cream. Lastly whisk the egg whites until they are very stiff, and, using a metal spoon, fold them quickly but thoroughly into the smoked trout mixture.

Pour into a bowl or ramekins to set. Decorate, if you wish, with finely chopped parsley, or thin slices of lemon, and serve with brown bread and butter.

69 Sardine and Mushroom Pâté

My husband loathes sardines, but loves this unusual pâté. It doesn't freeze very well, but can be kept in the fridge for 3–4 days.

Serves 6–8
75 g (3 oz) butter
225 g (8 oz) button mushrooms, wiped and sliced
2 × 120 g (4.2 oz) cans sardines, drained
225 g (8 oz) cream cheese
2–3 tbsp lemon juice
little salt and freshly ground black pepper

Melt the butter in a frying pan and sauté the mushrooms. Cool them, then mix with all the other ingredients in a food processor and whiz until smooth. If you don't have a food processor, use a pestle and mortar.

Pile into a serving dish and chill. Serve with wholemeal toast or bread.

70 Smoked Trout, Walnut and Cucumber Roulade

This is an unusual way of serving smoked trout, the crunchy textures of cucumber and crushed walnuts contrasting with the smooth cream cheese and fish.

Serves 6–8
575 ml (1 pt) milk
1 small onion, skinned and halved
1 bay leaf
a few peppercorns
50 g (2 oz) butter
50 g (2 oz) flour
4 eggs, separated
salt and freshly ground black pepper
freshly grated nutmeg
75 g (3 oz) walnuts, crushed
parsley to garnish (optional)
For the filling
2 smoked trout, flesh flaked from the bones
225 g (8 oz) cream cheese
150 ml (¼ pt) milk
2 tbsp lemon juice
salt and freshly ground black pepper
15 cm (6 in) length of cucumber, peeled, seeded and finely diced

First make the roulade. Put the milk, onion, bay leaf and peppercorns into a saucepan over a gentle heat. Infuse for 30 minutes. Then melt the butter in another saucepan, stir in the flour, cook for a minute or two, then gradually add the strained milk, stirring all the time until the sauce boils. Remove from the heat, season with salt, pepper and nutmeg and stir in the walnuts. Leave to cool for 10 minutes, then beat in the four egg yolks.

When the mixture is cold, whisk the egg whites until they are very stiff and, using a metal spoon, fold them in quickly but thoroughly. Line a Swiss roll tin, about 30 × 25 cm (12 × 10 in), with a piece of baking paper (siliconized greaseproof paper) and pour in the mixture. Bake in a moderate oven (180°C, 350°F, gas 4) for 20–25 minutes, until it feels firm to the touch.

Meanwhile make the filling. Put the cream cheese into a food processor or liquidizer and whiz, adding the milk to thin it a bit. Whiz in the lemon juice and seasoning then put the mixture into a bowl and stir in the trout and cucumber.

When the roulade is cooked take it out of the oven. Put a fresh piece of baking paper on to a work surface and tip the roulade on to it. Carefully peel the old paper off the back of the roulade. Roll it up, together with the paper it is lying on, and leave to get cold.

Unroll the roulade and spread the filling all over it. Roll it up again and put it on a serving dish. Sprinkle some finely chopped parsley over it before serving, if you like, and slice thickly like a Swiss roll to serve.

71 Mixed Seafood Mayonnaise

If the servings are increased this also makes a very good main course for a lunch or supper party.

Serves 6–8
450 g (1 lb) smoked haddock
450 g (1 lb) white fish fillet, cod or other
575 ml (1 pt) milk
575 ml (1 pt) water
1 onion, skinned and halved
1 blade of mace
142 ml (¼ pt) double cream, whipped
275 ml (½ pt) good mayonnaise
1 rounded tsp curry powder
1 tbsp lemon juice
1 rounded tbsp finely chopped parsley and chives, mixed
75 g (3 oz) cooked, shelled prawns
a few cooked mussels
iceberg or other crisp lettuce, washed and dried
50 g (2 oz) can anchovies, drained, soaked in milk for 30 minutes
*   and patted dry on absorbent paper*

Put the smoked and white fish into a saucepan together with the milk, water, onion and mace, and put the pan on a moderate heat. Bring the liquid slowly to simmering point and simmer very gently for 5 minutes, then draw the pan off the heat and cool the fish in the liquid. When cold flake the fish into a bowl, removing as many of the bones as you possibly can.

Mix together the whipped cream, mayonnaise, curry powder, lemon juice, parsley and chives. Stir in the flaked fish, prawns and mussels.

Shred the lettuce finely and place on a serving dish (or individual serving plates). Pile the fish in its creamy sauce on top and decorate with strips of anchovy fillet. Serve with brown bread and butter.

72 Fried Whitebait

These crispy deep-fried tiny fish are very easy to prepare, and need no more accompaniment than a dusting of cayenne pepper and a wedge of lemon.

Serves 6
700 g (1½ lb) whitebait (thawed if frozen)
oil for deep frying
75–125 g (3–4 oz) seasoned flour
lemon wedges
cayenne pepper

Heat the oil in a chip pan. Coat the whitebait thoroughly in seasoned flour. Cook them, a couple of handfuls at a time, until they are brown and crisp – about 3–4 minutes – then shake them from the oil and keep warm while you cook the rest.

Serve immediately with the lemon wedges and cayenne pepper.

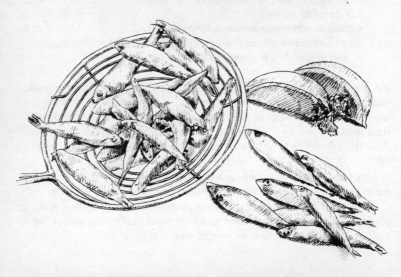

73 Crab and Avocado Salad

I love avocados, and they do seem to have a special affinity with shellfish. This makes a perfect first course for a summer evening, and is very easy and quick to put together.

Serves 6
450 g (1 lb) crabmeat, white and brown mixed
3 ripe avocados
4 tbsp good mayonnaise
2 tbsp lemon juice
salt and freshly ground black pepper
1 tbsp finely chopped chives and parsley, mixed

Mix together the mayonnaise, lemon juice, salt and pepper, parsley and chives. Stir in the crabmeat.

Cut each avocado in half, remove the stones, and carefully peel off the skin. I find this easier to do if I score it with the point of a very sharp knife and peel it off in thin strips. Put each avocado half, hole side down, on serving plates and cover with the crab mayonnaise. Serve with brown bread or rolls.

74 Sweet and Sour Herrings

Filleted herrings baked in a spicy sauce are among our favourites. They can be eaten hot or cold.

Serves 6
6 herrings, cleaned and filleted
2 tbsp oil
1 onion, finely chopped
1 tbsp wine vinegar
1 tbsp lemon juice
1 tbsp soft dark brown sugar
2 tbsp Worcestershire sauce
2 tbsp tomato ketchup

Put the herring fillets in an ovenproof dish. Heat the oil in a saucepan, add the finely chopped onion and cook for 5 minutes over a moderate heat, stirring occasionally, until the onion is soft and transparent. Stir in the other ingredients and pour the mixture over the herrings. Bake in a moderate oven (180°C, 350°F, gas 4) uncovered, for 20 minutes.

Serve hot or cold – I prefer them cold – with brown rolls or bread.

75 Shrimp Vol-Au-Vents

I think it's the combination of the puff pastry and the shrimps in their creamy sauce with the hint of nutmeg which makes these so irresistible. If you can't get shrimps you can substitute prawns, but cut them in half if they are very big. Allow 2 vol-au-vents per person.

Serves 6
12 × 5 cm (2 in) vol-au-vents, baked until well-risen and golden brown
For the sauce
450 g (1 lb) shrimps
50 g (2 oz) butter
50 g (2 oz) flour
575 ml (1 pt) milk
salt and freshly ground black pepper
freshly grated nutmeg

Melt the butter, stir in the flour and cook for a minute or two. Then gradually add the milk, stirring all the time until the sauce boils. Season with salt, pepper and nutmeg to taste. Stir in the shrimps and cook for long enough to heat them through. Put the warm vol-au-vents on the serving dishes and fill with shrimp sauce. Serve hot.

76 Prawn and Curry Cream Ramekins

This mousse, with all its variations, will be familiar to lots of people. Even without the prawns it is good; with them it is heavenly. It has the added bonus of being extremely easy and quick to make. Beware that there are two sorts of consommé on the market: one which has 'beef broth' in small letters under the word consommé which you don't want because it has no gelatine. The consommé which does have gelatine mentions the word 'jellied' somewhere on the tin.

Serves 6–8
2 × 400 g (14 oz) cans jellied consommé
2 garlic cloves skinned
2 tsp curry powder
225 g (8 oz) cream cheese
175 g (6 oz) prawns

Put the consommé, garlic, curry powder and cream cheese into the liquidizer and whiz until very smooth. Divide the prawns between the ramekins and pour the creamy mixture on top. Put them in the fridge to set.

Serve with brown bread or garlic bread.

77 Smoked Mackerel Pâté

Fat, juicy smoked mackerel can now be bought in most good food shops. You can eat them as they are, with a salad, but they also make up into one of the best of the smoked fish pâtés.

Serves 6–8
4 smoked mackerel fillets
225 g (8 oz) cream cheese
4 tbsp lemon juice
freshly ground black pepper
1 tbsp Worcestershire sauce
½ garlic clove, skinned and finely chopped
1 tbsp finely chopped parsley

Remove any bones you can find lurking in the smoked mackerel fillets, and put the fish into a food processor, together with the cream cheese, lemon juice, plenty of pepper, the Worcestershire sauce, garlic and parsley. (The parsley needs to be chopped first because otherwise it tends to remain in little clusters rather than get broken down finely.) If you don't have a food processor, use a pestle and mortar. Whiz or pound until you have a smooth mixture, then scoop the pâté into a serving dish and keep, covered, in the fridge until required.

Serve with warm brown toast.

78 *Shrimps with Brown Bread and Walnut Rolls*

This is the simplest way of all of serving shrimps, just with lemon juice squeezed over them, and lots of freshly ground black pepper. But in case you think it is a bit too simple, serve them with brown bread and walnut rolls.

Walnut rolls
sliced brown bread
chopped walnuts
butter, softened
salt

Cut the crusts off the bread and roll each slice with a rolling pin. This makes them easy to roll up; if you don't do it, the rolls crack.

Fry the walnuts in butter with some salt sprinkled over them, for 3–5 minutes, then drain and cool on absorbent paper. Spread the slices of bread with softened butter.

Sprinkle the walnuts as evenly as possible over each slice. Roll up lengthwise and cut each roll in half, so you have little rolls about 5 cm (2 in) long. Arrange them on a plate and keep, covered with cling film, until they are required.

79 Smoked Prawn Mayonnaise

A number of fish merchants now sell smoked prawns. They make an unusual first course folded into a creamy mayonnaise with just a hint of garlic, and served in individual glasses or dishes on a bed of finely shredded crisp lettuce.

Serves 6
450 g (1 lb) shelled smoked prawns
1 egg and 1 yolk
1 rounded tsp dry mustard
½ tsp salt
½ tsp caster sugar (optional)
½ tsp freshly ground black pepper
150 ml (¼ pt) sunflower seed oil
3 tbsp white wine vinegar
finely shredded lettuce
parsley to garnish (optional)

Put the egg, yolk, mustard powder, salt, sugar and pepper into a food processor or liquidizer. Whiz. Then, still whizzing, slowly add the oil, a dribble at a time, until it is all used up – the mayonnaise should be thick. Lastly whiz in the vinegar.

Mix the mayonnaise and prawns together, and divide between serving dishes one-third full of lettuce. Sprinkle with finely chopped parsley, if you like, before serving, and accompany with brown bread and butter.

M·A·I·N C·O·U·R·S·E·S F·O·R
E·V·E·R·Y D·A·Y

Fish Pie
Cod Baked with Onions, Tomatoes and Olives
Salt Herring
Smoked Haddock and Mushroom Vol-Au-Vents
Cod Steaks with Parsley Sauce
Gougère of Fish and Cheese
Smoked Haddock and Parsley Cream Tart
Smoked Haddock Soufflé
Grilled Lemon Sole with Hazelnut Butter
Fried Lemon Sole with Tomato Sauce
Lemon Sole with Parsley and Lemon Stuffing
Fish Lasagne
Peppered Smoked Mackerel and Brown Rice Salad
Fried Monkfish
Roast Monkfish Wrapped in Bacon
Indonesian-style Plaice
Plaice Stuffed with Hazelnuts
Plaice with Grapes and Cream
Grilled Plaice with Mushroom Sauce
Fish Goulash
Skate with Black Butter
Fish Florentine
Whiting with Oatmeal, Garlic and Parsley
Mussel and Tomato Spaghetti Sauce
Sardine, Tomato and Pepper Sauce for Spaghetti
Cheese, Bacon and Cod Spaghetti Sauce
Normandy Cod Casserole
Cod Provençale
Cod, Mushroom and Bacon Kebabs
Hake with Mushrooms, Cream and Soya Sauce

Invergarry Crab Cakes
Baked Plaice with Onions, Tomatoes and White Wine
Tuna Fish in Hot Creamy Mayonnaise Sauce
Tuna Fish and Pasta Salad
Fresh Pilchards and Sardines
Cod with Garlic Butter and Almonds
Spinach, Cod and Cheese Roulade
Baked Sole with Capers and Lemon Juice
John Dory Fillets Baked with Mushrooms and Sherry
Baked Bream with Garlic and Peppers
Lemon Baked Red Mullet
Baked Bass with Lemon and Parsley Stuffing
Bass Baked with Tomato and Fennel

80 *Fish Pie*

So often the words fish pie conjure up in people's minds dreadful memories of ghastly school dinner. It is sad but true that institutional cooks can positively vandalize certain dishes, and fish pie is one of them. A really good fish pie is one of the most delicious of all dishes.

Fish pie is so versatile. It can be simply made from smoked and white fish with mashed potato on top, or dressed up and rendered worthy of a dinner party by adding a few prawns and a dash of white wine to the sauce, and substituting a puffed pastry top.

This is a recipe for an everyday pie.

Serves 6–8
700 g (1½ lb) haddock, cod or other white fish
700 g (1½ lb) smoked haddock or cod
1.1 litres (2 pt) milk
1 onion, skinned
1 blade of mace (optional)
75 g (3 oz) butter
75 g (3 oz) plain flour
50 g (2 oz) Cheddar or Lancashire cheese, grated
3 tomatoes, skinned, seeded and chopped
salt and freshly ground black pepper
2 hard-boiled eggs, shelled and chopped
2 rounded tbsp finely chopped parsley
about 900 g (2 lb) potatoes, freshly boiled and mashed

Put the fish, milk, onion and mace together in a saucepan and, over a gentle heat, bring slowly to the boil. Simmer for 2 minutes, then remove the pan from the heat and let the fish cool in the milk. Strain off the milk, when cool, keeping it in a jug to make the sauce. Flake the fish, removing the bones and skin.

Melt the butter in a saucepan and stir in the flour. Cook for a minute or two, stirring, then gradually pour on the reserved milk, stirring the sauce all the time until it boils. Take it off the heat and stir in the cheese, the fish, the hard-boiled egg and tomatoes. Season with a very little salt and lots of pepper. Pour this all into a 2.3 litre (4 pt) ovenproof dish and leave. Arrange the mashed potatoes on top and bake in a moderate oven (180°C, 350°F, gas 4) for about 40 minutes, until the sauce underneath the potato is bubbling, and a golden crust has formed on top.

81 Cod Baked with Onions, Tomatoes and Olives

This is an ideal dish for those who, like me, are watching their calorie intake. It is nicest if eaten freshly made, but it is nearly as good if made in the morning and reheated for dinner that night.

Serves 6
900 g (2 lb) cod fillet
3 tbsp sunflower oil
1 large or 2 small onions, skinned and finely sliced
2 × 425 g (15 oz) cans tomatoes
pinch of sugar
salt and freshly ground black pepper
1 tsp chopped fresh basil, or ½ tsp dried basil
50 g (2 oz) large juicy green olives, stoned and roughly chopped

Cut the cod into chunks about 2.5 cm (1 in) in size. Set on one side.

Heat the oil in a casserole and add the onions. Cook over a gentle heat for 5 minutes, stirring occasionally, until the onions are soft and transparent. Stir in the tomatoes, sugar, salt, plenty of pepper and the dried basil if you are using it – if you are using fresh add that just before serving. Simmer the sauce, uncovered, for 40–45 minutes; it will reduce and thicken as it simmers.

Add the olives and the chunks of cod. Cover the casserole and simmer very gently for about 15 minutes or until the pieces of fish are cooked but not falling apart.

Serve with boiled brown rice and a green vegetable like broccoli, or a green salad.

82 *Salt Herring*

If you get the chance of buying salt herring do try it if you haven't already. Allow 2 salt herring per person.

Wash and rinse the herring very well under running cold water. Put them into a bowl covered with cold water for 3–4 hours, changing the water twice. Then put them into a large saucepan and cover with fresh cold water. Bring slowly to the boil, drain, cover with fresh cold water, bring slowly to the boil again, and simmer gently for 5 minutes.

Drain and serve with plain boiled potatoes. If you like, you can make a third change of water during the cooking time to make them less salty.

83 Smoked Haddock and Mushroom Vol-Au-Vents

Our children love these for lunch or supper. Actually they love *anything* in vol-au-vent cases, but the smoked haddock and mushroom filling seems to be especially popular. It is convenient, too, because the sauce can be made ahead of time, and the vol-au-vents baked and the sauce heated just before serving.

Serves 6
12 medium vol-au-vent cases
450 g (1 lb) smoked haddock
0.8 litre (1½ pt) milk
50 g (2 oz) butter
50 g (2 oz) flour
salt and freshly ground black pepper
3 tbsp oil
225 g (8 oz) button mushrooms, wiped and sliced
50 g (2 oz) grated cheese

Put the smoked haddock into a saucepan together with the milk. Put the saucepan over a moderate heat and bring the milk slowly to simmering point. Simmer gently for 5 minutes, then draw the pan off the heat and leave the fish to cool in the liquid.

Melt the butter in a saucepan and stir in the flour. Cook for a minute or two, then gradually strain in the milk in which the fish cooked, stirring all the time, until the sauce boils. Draw the pan off the heat and stir in the cheese, a little salt and pepper to taste. Flake the cooked smoked haddock into the sauce, removing any skin and bones.

Heat the oil in a frying pan or saucepan and add the mushrooms. Cook over a high heat for 2–3 minutes, stirring them around – a high heat stops them from shrinking so much. Using a slotted spoon to drain off any liquid, remove the mushrooms from the pan and add them to the smoked haddock sauce.

When you are ready to serve, bake the vol-au-vent cases in a hot oven until they are golden brown and well puffed up. Put two on each serving plate and fill to overflowing with the sauce.

84 Cod Steaks with Parsley Sauce

Really fresh cod is so good I like simply to grill it under a grill which is only on about three-quarters of its full temperature. If it is red-hot the fish tends to become dry and hard on top, no matter how carefully you baste it with melted butter. Serve with a white sauce full of finely chopped parsley, which I stir into the sauce at the last minute, so that it retains its fresh flavour and colour, which tend to go if it is added too far ahead.

Serves 6
6 cod steaks, or pieces of cod fillet
175 g (6 oz) butter or polyunsaturated margarine
salt and freshly ground black pepper
6 lemon wedges to serve (optional)
For the sauce
50 g (2 oz) butter
50 g (2 oz) wholemeal or plain flour
575 ml (1 pt) milk
salt and freshly ground black pepper
freshly grated nutmeg
2 heaped tbsp finely chopped parsley

First make the sauce. Melt the butter in a saucepan and stir in the flour. Cook for a couple of minutes, stirring occasionally, then gradually add the milk, stirring all the time until it comes to the boil. Stir, as the sauce bubbles, for a minute, then draw the sauce off the heat and season with the salt, pepper and nutmeg. Just before serving, stir in the finely chopped parsley.

Heat the grill to medium. Put the pieces of fish on to a baking tray and top each one with a piece of the butter. Season lightly with salt and pepper and put under the grill. As the butter melts, brush the fish with it from time to time as it cooks. The fish will take about 7–10 minutes to cook, depending on its thickness.

Serve immediately, and either hand the parsley sauce round separately, or pour it over each piece of fish. Serve a lemon wedge beside each portion if not covered with the sauce.

I like to serve creamy mashed potatoes with this, and perhaps parsnips and carrots, cooked together – I think parsnips go very well with fish.

85 Gougère of Fish and Cheese

You can use any sort of fish for this dish, but as I personally love smoked fish, I tend to use a mixture of smoked haddock and either cod or fresh haddock. Gougère is a crisp, cheesy choux pastry, spooned around the sides of an ovenproof dish, with the fish in a cheesy sauce in the middle. It freezes well. Make the gougère mixture, put it round the sides and over the bottom of the dish, pour in the cooled fishy sauce and freeze. If it is thawed for a couple of hours, then baked as in the recipe, it is very convenient as well as delicious.

Serves 6
For the gougère
200 ml (7 fl oz) water
75 g (3 oz) butter
125 g (4 oz) strong plain flour, sieved with 1 rounded tsp dry mustard
4 large eggs
salt and freshly ground black pepper
75 g (3 oz) grated cheese
For the filling
450 g (1 lb) smoked haddock
450 g (1 lb) cod or fresh haddock
0.8 litre (1½ pt) milk
1 onion, skinned
1 blade of mace
a few black peppercorns
50 g (2 oz) butter
50 g (2 oz) flour
50 g (2 oz) grated cheese

Put the water into a saucepan and cut up the butter into it. Put the pan over a moderate heat and when the butter has melted let the liquid just come to the boil. Take the pan off the heat and beat in the flour and mustard, beating hard until the mixture comes away from the sides of the pan. Leave to cool for 10 minutes.

Beat in the eggs, one by one, beating until they are all used up and the mixture is smooth and glossy. Season with a little salt and plenty of pepper and beat in the cheese. Butter an ovenproof dish and spoon the cheesy choux pastry around the sides and thinly over the bottom.

Next make the filling. Put the fish together in a saucepan with the milk, onion, mace and peppercorns. Put the saucepan over a moderate heat and bring the liquid slowly to the boil. Simmer gently for 5 minutes, then draw the pan off the heat and let the fish cool in the liquid. When cool, strain the milk off into a jug.

Melt the butter in a saucepan and stir in the flour. Cook for a minute or two, then gradually add the strained milk, stirring until the sauce boils. Season with pepper (salt should not be necessary) and draw the pan off the heat.

Flake the cooled fish, removing the skin and bones, and stir the flesh into the sauce. Pour the sauce into the middle of the gougère, and sprinkle the cheese over the top of sauce and pastry. Bake in a moderately hot oven (200°C, 400°F, gas 6) for about 20–25 minutes, until the pastry is well risen and golden brown. Serve immediately.

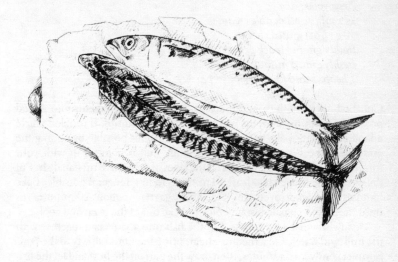

86 Smoked Haddock and Parsley Cream Tart

This tart is good for lunch, supper or picnics at any time of the year.

Serves 6–8
100 g (3½ oz) butter, hard from the fridge
175 g (6 oz) flour
2 tsp icing sugar
½ tsp salt
For the filling
700 g (1½ lb) smoked haddock
0.8 litre (1½ pt) milk and water mixed
2 eggs
2 egg yolks
275 ml (½ pt) double cream
50 g (2 oz) grated cheese
freshly ground black pepper
freshly grated nutmeg
1 heaped tbsp finely chopped parsley

Cut the butter into bits, and put it and the other ingredients into a food processor, and whiz until the mixture is like fine crumbs. If you don't have a food processor, make the pastry as crumb-like as possible by cutting the butter into the mixture with a sharp knife and rubbing it in with your fingers. Then pat it into and around the sides of a 20 cm (8 in) flan dish. Put the dish in the fridge for at least 30 minutes to rest; longer if possible. Bake blind in a moderate oven (180°C, 350°F, gas 4) for about 20 minutes, or until the pastry is a pale biscuit colour. Take out of the oven and cool.

Meanwhile make the filling. Put the fish into a saucepan together with the milk and water. On a medium heat, bring the liquid slowly to the boil. Simmer gently for 5 minutes, then draw the pan off the heat and let the fish cool in the liquid.

Beat together the eggs, egg yolks, cream, cheese and 275 ml (½ pt) of the fish liquid. Season to taste with pepper and nutmeg. Flake the cooled fish from the bones and skin and stir the flaked fish into the egg mixture. Stir in the parsley and pour the mixture into the cooked pastry case. Bake in a moderate oven (180°C, 350°F, gas 4) for 25–30 minutes, until the filling is just firm to the touch.

Take out of the oven and serve warm or cold – it's nicest warm – with a mixed green salad and warm brown rolls.

87 Smoked Haddock Soufflé

For many people soufflés have a sort of culinary mystique. They had for me, too, until several years ago I tackled a cheese soufflé. To my surprise and delight it turned out magnificently, was easy to make, and brought cries of glee from my husband and visiting parents. The snag about soufflés is that they *must* be eaten as soon as they come out of the oven, so I rarely make them for more than six people – any more and there is bound to be someone who just has to nip upstairs and fetch something and so holds up the rest, and in the waiting my beautiful, lofty soufflé slowly but resolutely sinks, and there is nothing at all to be done about it!

This smoked haddock soufflé goes well with Fresh tomato sauce (rec. 29), handed separately.

Serves 4–6
700 g (1½ lb) smoked haddock
0.8 litre (1½ pt) milk
75 g (3 oz) butter
75 g (3 oz) plain flour
75 g (3 oz) grated cheese
freshly ground black pepper
freshly grated nutmeg
6 large eggs, separated

Butter a soufflé dish about 25 cm (10 in) in diameter.

Put the smoked haddock and milk into a saucepan and put the pan on a moderate heat. Bring the milk slowly to the boil, simmer gently for 5 minutes, then draw the pan off the heat and let the fish cool in the milk for 20 minutes or so. Strain the milk off the fish and reserve it for the sauce. When the fish is cool enough to handle flake it off the skin, removing any bones.

Melt the butter in a saucepan and stir in the flour. Cook for a minute or two, stirring occasionally. Then, stirring continuously, add the reserved milk, stirring until the sauce boils. Draw the pan off the heat and stir in the grated cheese, black pepper and nutmeg. Beat the egg yolks one by one into the sauce mixture. Stir in the flaked fish and leave to cool.

About 45 minutes before you are ready to eat whisk the whites until very stiff, and using a large metal spoon fold them quickly but thoroughly into the sauce. Pour into the buttered soufflé dish and bake in a hot oven (220°C, 425°F, gas 7). The soufflé will take about 40 minutes to cook; serve immediately.

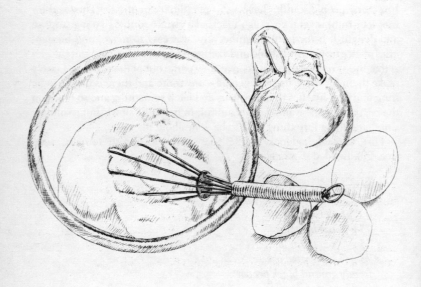

88 *Grilled Lemon Sole with Hazelnut Butter*

As with all fish, lemon sole is at its best absolutely fresh. When grilled it is one of the quickest meals there is, provided that you have its accompanying vegetables ready. It is also a very good meal for calorie counters. Serve with either a plain wedge of lemon or, more interestingly, a Fresh tomato sauce (rec. 29).

I allow one good-sized lemon sole per person. Put them on a baking tray, dot with butter and squeeze over some lemon juice, and put under a medium-hot grill (not full on, because the fish tends to harden on the outside during cooking). They will only take about 5 minutes to cook.

For those not bothered by weight-watching problems, hazelnut butter is delicious with grilled lemon sole – and with all other grilled or poached fish.

Hazelnut butter
125 g (4 oz) butter
25 g (1 oz) ground hazelnuts

I like to toast the hazelnuts – I love the flavour of toasted nuts. Just put them into a dry saucepan, over a moderate heat, and shake the pan to prevent them burning. Cook for about 5 minutes and leave to cool.

Beat the butter until creamy, then beat in the nuts. Roll up into a fat sausage shape in greaseproof paper and keep in the fridge. To serve cut off a fairly thick slice and put one on top of each portion of fish.

89 Fried Lemon Sole with Tomato Sauce

This is an ideal lunch for children, but adults love it too. I allow one lemon sole per person.

Dip the filleted soles into a bowl of beaten egg, then into a bowl of wholemeal breadcrumbs.

Heat about 4 tablespoons of oil in a large shallow pan. When the oil sizzles when you drop a few breadcrumbs in it, put in the fish, and fry for 2–3 minutes on each side. If necessary keep the first fish hot on a dish lined with absorbent paper while you cook the remainder.

Serve with Fresh tomato sauce (rec. 29), handed separately.

90 *Lemon Sole with Parsley and Lemon Stuffing*

For this recipe you need fillets of sole, which is how sole is to be found in most fish shops anyway. The pieces of fish are rolled around the stuffing and baked in a light parsley sauce. They are nicest eaten straight from the oven, but you can prepare the fish and make the sauce in the morning, putting them together and baking in the evening.

Serves 6
2 sole fillets per person
50 g (2 oz) butter
1 small onion, very finely chopped
125 g (4 oz) wholemeal breadcrumbs
grated rind of 1 lemon
salt and freshly ground black pepper
1 heaped tbsp finely chopped parsley
For the sauce
50 g (2 oz) butter
1 rounded tbsp flour
575 ml (1 pt) milk
salt and freshly ground black pepper
freshly grated nutmeg
2 rounded tbsp finely chopped parsley

Start by making the stuffing. Melt the butter in a shallow pan or frying pan. Add the onion and cook over a gentle heat, stirring occasionally, for about 5 minutes, when the onion should be soft and transparent. Stir in the breadcrumbs, lemon rind, a little salt, plenty of pepper and the parsley. Cook for a further 5 minutes, then put on one side to cool.

When cool enough to handle, squeeze the stuffing together and divide evenly between each sole fillet. Roll each piece of fish around the stuffing and secure with a wooden cocktail stick. Put the rolls into a buttered ovenproof dish.

Then make the sauce. Melt the butter in a saucepan and stir in the flour. Cook for a couple of minutes, stirring from time to time, then gradually add the milk, stirring all the time until the sauce boils. Draw the pan off the heat and season to taste with a little salt, freshly ground black pepper and nutmeg. Stir in the parsley and pour the sauce over the rolled-up fish.

Cover with a piece of foil and bake in a moderate oven (180°C, 350°F, gas 4), for 45 minutes – the sauce will be bubbling. Serve immediately.

This is good served with brown rice and a green salad.

91 Fish Lasagne

This is a most convenient dish to make as it can be put together in the morning or the day before, and baked just before the meal. I put just one layer of tomato sauce in the middle, as any more makes the tomato taste too marked. I make it with smoked haddock, but it could be dressed up with prawns and crab into a real dinner-party dish.

Serves 6–8
900 g (2 lb) smoked haddock
1.7 litres (3 pt) milk
1 onion, skinned
1 stick of celery
75 g (3 oz) butter
75 g (3 oz) wholemeal or plain flour
freshly ground black pepper
freshly grated nutmeg
125 g (4 oz) grated cheese
about 225 g (8 oz) ready-to-bake lasagne or lasagne verdi
about 275 ml (½ pt) Fresh tomato sauce (rec. 29)

Butter a fairly shallow ovenproof dish. Put the smoked haddock, milk, onion and celery together in a saucepan and put the pan over a medium heat. Bring the milk slowly to the boil, and simmer very gently for about 5 minutes. Then draw the pan off the heat and let the fish cool in the milk. When the fish is nearly cold, strain the milk into a jug for the sauce. Flake the fish, removing the skin and bones, and keep on one side.

Make the sauce by melting the butter in a saucepan and stirring in the flour. Cook for a minute or two, stirring occasionally, then gradually add the fishy milk, stirring all the time, until the sauce boils. It should be fairly runny. Draw the pan off the heat. Season with pepper and nutmeg. Stir in three-quarters of the grated cheese, reserving a quarter to go on top, then the flaked fish.

Pour a layer of the fishy sauce over the bottom of the buttered ovenproof dish, and arrange a layer of lasagne on top. Layer again with the sauce and lasagne, then pour in the tomato sauce followed by lasagne. Continue layering like this until the sauce is all used up, ending with a layer of sauce. Sprinkle with the reserved grated cheese and leave until you are ready to bake it. Bake in a moderate oven (180°C, 350°F, gas 4) for 45 minutes. The sauce will be bubbling and the grated cheese melted and golden brown.

Serve with garlic-buttered rolls and a salad.

92 *Peppered Smoked Mackerel and Brown Rice Salad*

This is a perfect dish for a summer lunch. Fillets of smoked mackerel coated with crushed black peppercorns can be bought in most fish shops and good food departments. When flaked into a mixture of brown rice, chopped hard-boiled eggs and plenty of chopped chives and parsley, and all mixed into a slightly mustardy yoghurt sauce which counteracts the richness of the mackerel, the result is superb.

Serves 6–8
6 fillets of peppered mackerel, flesh flaked and bones removed
2 tsp grainy mustard
2 tbsp mayonnaise
150 g (5 oz) natural yoghurt
225 g (8 oz) brown rice, boiled until cooked but still with a slightly nutty crunch
3 hard-boiled eggs, shelled and chopped
3 heaped tbsp chopped chives and parsley mixed
tomatoes, quartered (optional)

Stir the mustard, mayonnaise and yoghurt together. Fold together the rice, the flaked mackerel and the hard-boiled egg, together with most of the chopped parsley and chives. Fold the mustardy sauce into the fishy rice mixture and heap on to a flat serving dish.

Press wedges of tomato around the sides of the rice, if you like. Sprinkle the remaining chives and parsley over the top.

93 Fried Monkfish

A whole monkfish is a fearsome object, but usually one finds just the tail for sale in fish shops. Restaurants of dubious reputation pass off pieces of monkfish as large prawns, which gives you some idea of what cooked monkfish is like – well worth seeking out. I like just to cut the tail in rounds and fry them gently in butter.

Serves 6
about 1.4 kg (3 lb) monkfish, cut in 2.5 cm (1 in) thick slices
2 tbsp wholemeal flour
freshly ground black pepper
75 g (3 oz) butter and 1 tbsp oil
2 garlic cloves, skinned and finely chopped
1 heaped tbsp finely chopped parsley
juice of 1 lemon

Heat the butter and oil together in a wide, shallow pan, a frying pan is ideal. Dip each piece of monkfish in the wholemeal flour seasoned with pepper and fry in the hot butter and oil for about 3–4 minutes. Halfway through, add the garlic and turn the pieces of monkfish over so that they cook on both sides. Sprinkle the parsley into the pan and when the pieces of fish are cooked squeeze the lemon juice over them.

Serve hot: I like it with brown rice and fennel or celery. Any of the sauces in the sauces chapter would be an enhancement, although there is plenty of flavour in the monkfish just like this.

94 Roast Monkfish Wrapped in Bacon

Monkfish has firm, succulent flesh; the bacon keeps it moist while cooking, while the flavours of bacon and fish – particularly shellfish, which monkfish resembles – complement each other well. You can serve a rich sauce with this, such as hollandaise, but I prefer it with Fresh tomato sauce (rec. 29).

Serves 6
1.4 kg (3 lb) monkfish tail
thinly cut rashers of streaky bacon

Trim the monkfish. Cut off the membrane from the outside of the fish, and cut the flesh away from the backbone. (Use this to make some fish stock and freeze it.)

Wrap the fillets of monkfish in bacon rashers and place in a roasting tin. Roast in a moderate oven (190°C, 375°F, gas 5) for 25–30 minutes.

Cut into thickish slices to serve, handing the sauce separately.

95 *Indonesian-style Plaice*

Fish with curry, coconut and bananas may sound an odd combination, but
it is very good. As the fillets of plaice are fried the coconut and curry powder
coating forms a splendid crispness around them, and fried bananas make a
perfect accompaniment. I usually serve this with boiled brown rice and a
mixed salad.

Serves 6
1 plaice per person, filleted
1 egg, beaten, on a plate
4 tbsp desiccated coconut, mixed with
  1 tbsp mild curry powder
3 large bananas, peeled and cut in half lengthwise and across
4 tbsp oil
6 lemon wedges

Dip each piece of fish in the beaten egg, then in the curry and coconut
mixture. Heat the oil in a frying pan, and fry the coconut-coated pieces of
fish, turning each over carefully so that it cooks on both sides.

Cook the bananas in the same frying pan, if there is room. If not, keep
the pieces of fish hot on an ovenproof dish lined with absorbent paper while
you then fry the bananas. Serve immediately, with the lemon wedges.

96 *Plaice Stuffed with Hazelnuts*

Stuffed and rolled fish fillets have a tendency to come unrolled during cooking, but I find that leaving them in the fridge for 15 minutes or so first prevents this. The hazelnuts go very well with the fish, and the lemon juice adds that touch of sharpness. You can cook lemon sole fillets in the same way.

Serves 6
12 fillets of plaice
50 g (2 oz) butter
1 onion, skinned and very finely chopped
125 g (4 oz) ground hazelnuts
3–4 tbsp wholemeal breadcrumbs
1 tbsp finely chopped parsley
2 tbsp seasoned flour
beaten egg
oil for frying
juice of 1 lemon

Melt the butter in a saucepan and add the finely chopped onion. Cook over a moderate heat for 5 minutes, then add the hazelnuts and cook for a further 5 minutes, stirring occasionally to prevent sticking. Stir in 1 tablespoon of the breadcrumbs and the parsley and leave to cool.

Divide the stuffing evenly between the 12 fillets. Roll up and dip each roll in the seasoned flour, then the beaten egg, then the remaining breadcrumbs. Heat some oil in a frying pan and fry the rolls, turning carefully to ensure they cook evenly all over.

Pour the lemon juice over the rolls and serve immediately.

97 Plaice with Grapes and Cream

Although I much prefer plaice, this rich but simple dish can be made equally well with lemon sole.

Serves 6
6 plaice, either filleted or on the bone
about 10 g (½ oz) butter on each fish
284 ml (½ pt) double cream
juice of ½ lemon
125 g (4 oz) green grapes, halved and seeded
salt and freshly ground pepper

Put the plaice on a baking sheet, dot with the butter (don't season as salt tends to toughen the fish) and put under a medium-hot grill for 4–5 minutes until cooked. Remove to a large, warmed serving dish.

Meanwhile pour the cream into a saucepan and add the grapes. Bring the cream to a gentle boil and simmer for 2–3 minutes, then stir in the lemon juice and a pinch of salt and pepper. Pour the sauce over the fish, and serve hot.

This is good with creamy mashed potatoes and fresh young peas.

98 Grilled Plaice with Mushroom Sauce

This recipe makes for a rather less rich dish than the previous one. I make the mushroom sauce, as I do many others, with wholemeal flour which gives a very slightly nutty taste.

Serves 6
6 plaice, either filleted or on the bone
about 10 g (½ oz) butter on each fish
For the mushroom sauce
50 g (2 oz) butter
1 small onion, skinned and finely chopped
225 g (8 oz) button mushrooms, wiped and sliced
1 rounded tbsp wholemeal or plain flour
425–575 ml (¾–1 pt) milk
salt and freshly ground black pepper
freshly grated nutmeg
1–2 tbsp finely chopped parsley

Start by making the mushroom sauce. Melt the butter in a saucepan and add the onion. Cook for 5 minutes, stirring occasionally, then add the mushrooms. Cook for a minute or two, then stir in the flour. Cook for a further 2–3 minutes, stirring occasionally, then gradually add the milk, stirring continuously until the sauce boils. Use enough to make a fairly thick sauce. Season with salt, pepper and nutmeg.

Put the fish on a baking tray, top each with a piece of butter and put under a medium-hot grill. The fish will take about 5 minutes to cook. Sprinkle a little parsley on each fish before serving and hand the mushroom sauce separately.

99 *Fish Goulash*

Goulash is a very good dish for the figure-conscious, because it is really just a thick stew of peppers, onions and tomatoes (thickened only by reducing during cooking) with the chunks of firm, white fish in it. I like to serve it with brown rice and a green salad.

Serves 6
900 g (2 lb) cod or other firm white fish
3 tbsp oil, preferably olive
2 medium onions, skinned and finely sliced
3 red and 2 green peppers, seeded and sliced
1 tbsp tomato purée
6 tomatoes, skinned, seeded and chopped
2 tsp paprika
½ tsp sugar
salt and freshly ground black pepper
½ carton natural yoghurt

Cut the fish into chunks about 2.5 cm (1 in) in size. Heat the oil in a large casserole and add the onions. Cook for 5 minutes, stirring occasionally, until the onions are soft and transparent. Add the peppers and cook for a further 5 minutes, stirring from time to time. Stir in the tomato purée, tomatoes, paprika, sugar, a pinch of salt and plenty of pepper. Cook, uncovered, over a gentle heat, stirring occasionally, for 30 minutes.

Add the chunks of fish, cover and cook for a further 20 minutes. Just before serving pour the yoghurt over the contents of the casserole.

100 *Skate with Black Butter*

A whole skate is a rather daunting sight, but it is usually bought by the 'wing'. One of these, weighing about 900 g (2 lb), is plenty for 4 people. Skate is very gelatinous and moist – or it should be; if it is dry, it is not fresh. It has ridges of soft gristle-like bone, and the flesh is translucent-white and succulent. Traditionally it is cooked in a court bouillon and served with *beurre noir*, black butter, which is very easy to make.

Serves 4
1 wing of skate
For the court bouillon
1.1 litres (2 pt) water
1 tsp salt
a few black peppercorns
125 ml (4 fl oz) dry white wine
1 large onion, skinned and thinly sliced
a few parsley stalks
For the beurre noir
50 g (2 oz) butter
lemon juice
finely chopped parsley
chopped capers (optional)

Put the court bouillon ingredients into a large saucepan, bring to the boil and simmer for 5 minutes. Put the skate wing in a roasting tin and pour the court bouillon over. Bake in a moderate oven (180°C, 350°F, gas 4) for 25–30 minutes. When the liquid is just simmering cover the tin with a piece of foil for the remaining cooking time.

To make the *beurre noir* melt the butter and cook until it is brown – not black, because it will then taste burnt. Add a squeeze of lemon juice and some finely chopped parsley, and, if you like, some chopped capers. Take the skate off the bone. Pour the butter sauce over the skate before serving.

101 Fish Florentine

This recipe is a favourite with everyone in our family. It is a variation on the classic dish, eggs Florentine, using fish instead of eggs, and one of those useful dishes in which the vegetables and fish all cook together. I think the ideal accompaniment is brown wholemeal rolls, generously spread with garlic butter, wrapped in foil and heated in the oven until the butter has melted into the bread.

Serves 6
12 fillets of plaice or lemon sole
0.8 litre (1½ pt) milk
1 onion, skinned
blade of mace
700 g (1½ lb) frozen chopped spinach, thawed
50 g (2 oz) butter
salt and freshly ground black pepper
freshly grated nutmeg
For the sauce
50 g (2 oz) butter
50 g (2 oz) wholemeal or plain flour
the milk the fish cooked in
125 g (4 oz) good strong Cheddar or Lancashire cheese
1 rounded tsp English mustard

Put the fish in a saucepan with the milk, onion and mace. Put the pan over a gentle to moderate heat, and bring the milk just to the boil then remove the saucepan from the heat, and let the fish cool in the milk. Gently lift the cooled fish out of the milk, and flake it.

Squeeze as much water out of the thawed spinach as you can. Melt the butter in a saucepan, add the spinach, salt, pepper and nutmeg, cover, and cook gently for about 10 minutes, stirring from time to time. Then put the spinach into a food processor or liquidizer and whiz to a purée. Put the puréed spinach into the bottom of a well-buttered ovenproof dish.

Next make the sauce. Melt the butter in a saucepan, add the flour and cook for a couple of minutes, stirring occasionally. Gradually add the milk the fish cooked in, stirring all the time until the sauce boils. Then draw the saucepan off the heat, and stir in about three-quarters of the grated cheese. Season with salt, pepper and the mustard.

Put the flaked fish on top of the spinach and pour the cheese sauce over. Sprinkle with the remaining grated cheese and bake in a moderate oven (180°C, 350°F, gas 4) for 20–30 minutes, until the sauce is bubbling and the cheese on top has melted. Serve immediately.

102 Whiting with Oatmeal, Garlic and Parsley

This is a very economical dish which takes just a few minutes to cook and tastes extremely good. I love the contrasting crunch of the fried oatmeal.

Serves 6
12 fillets of whiting
50 g (2 oz) butter and 1 tbsp oil
50 g (2 oz) oatmeal
salt and freshly ground black pepper
1 heaped tbsp chopped parsley
1 garlic clove, skinned and very finely chopped

Heat the butter and oil in a frying pan. Add the whiting fillets and sprinkle the oatmeal over them. Fry over a moderate heat, turning the fillets after 3–4 minutes so that they cook on both sides. Remove the fillets to an ovenproof dish and keep warm. Continue to fry the oatmeal, adding the garlic. Just before serving add the parsley. Cook for a minute or two, then pour the crunchy oatmeal mixture over the cooked fillets and serve.

103 Mussel and Tomato Spaghetti Sauce

This makes a lovely sauce to eat with spaghetti or tagliatelle. You can either take off half of each mussel shell, or remove the mussels from their shells entirely – this makes for less messy eating, but leaving half of the shell looks more attractive.

Serves 6
1.7 litres (3 pt) mussels, scrubbed under running cold water
275 ml (½ pt) white wine
275 ml (½ pt) water
1 large garlic clove, skinned and chopped
chopped parsley to serve
For the sauce
2 tbsp olive oil
1 large onion, skinned and finely chopped
1 garlic clove, skinned and finely chopped
700 g (1½ lb) fresh tomatoes, skinned, seeded and chopped; or
    2 × 425 g (15 oz) cans tomatoes
½ tsp sugar
½ tsp salt
freshly ground black pepper
fresh basil, chopped or snipped

Start by making the sauce. Heat the oil in a saucepan and add the chopped onion. Cook over a medium heat for 5 minutes, stirring occasionally, until the onion is soft and transparent. Then add the garlic, tomatoes, sugar, salt and plenty of pepper. Simmer gently, uncovered, for 35–40 minutes.

Meanwhile put the mussels into a saucepan with the wine, water and garlic. Cover and put on a fairly high heat. Cook for 7–10 minutes, shaking the pan from time to time, then remove from the heat. Cool until the mussels can be handled without causing you agony, and throw away any unopened ones. Either take the mussels out of their shells entirely, or throw away half their shell. Stir them into the tomato sauce, together with the basil, and serve with spaghetti or tagliatelle, generously sprinkled with parsley.

104 Sardine, Tomato and Pepper Sauce for Spaghetti

One of Caroline Fox's inventions, this spaghetti is as delicious as it is quick
to put together, and also qualifies as a panic meal: one of those meals
thrown together from the contents of the store cupboard when you are
suddenly confronted with unexpected guests. On such occasions the red
pepper can be replaced by tinned pimentos.

Serves 4–6
2 tbsp olive oil
1 large red pepper, seeded and quite finely chopped
2 × 425 g (15 oz) cans tomatoes
3 × 120 g (4.2 oz) cans sardines, drained
salt and freshly ground black pepper
2 tbsp chopped parsley

Heat the oil in a large saucepan and add the red pepper. Cook for 3–5
minutes, then add the tomatoes, sardines, a pinch of salt and plenty of
pepper. Simmer for 20 minutes, stirring occasionally to prevent sticking
and to break up the tomatoes and sardines.

Serve with spaghetti or tagliatelle, lavishly sprinkled with parsley.

105 Cheese, Bacon and Cod Spaghetti Sauce

This is another sauce for serving with pasta. It is fairly filling, and can be made into a macaroni pie if the sauce is stirred into cooked macaroni, poured into a buttered ovenproof dish, then sprinkled with grated cheese and baked. Or you can serve it separately from the pasta.

I love the combination of bacon and fish – any fish or shellfish seems to be complemented by it. You can substitute any firm-fleshed white fish for the cod, or you can use tuna fish.

Serves 4–6
450 g (1 lb) cod fillets
0.8 litre (1½ pt) milk
1 onion, skinned
1 stick of celery
For the sauce
4 rashers smoked bacon, coarsely chopped
1 small onion, skinned and finely chopped
50 g (2 oz) butter
50 g (2 oz) wholemeal or plain flour
the milk the fish cooked in
125 g (4 oz) grated Cheddar or Lancashire cheese
salt and freshly ground black pepper

Put the cod into a saucepan together with the milk, onion and celery. Put the pan over a medium heat and bring the milk gently to the boil. Simmer gently for 3–5 minutes, then draw the pan off the heat and let the fish cool in the milk. Then strain the milk into a jug and flake the fish, removing any bones that happen to be lurking. Set the fish aside while you make the sauce.

Melt the butter in a saucepan and add the bacon and onion. Cook for 5–10 minutes, stirring occasionally to prevent sticking. The bacon should turn crisp and the onion soft and golden brown. Then stir in the flour and cook for a further minute or two. Gradually add the fishy milk, stirring all the time until the sauce boils. Draw the pan off the heat and stir in the grated cheese, a pinch of salt and pepper to taste. Stir in the flaked fish and serve with cooked pasta.

106 Normandy Cod Casserole

Fish goes very well with apples and cider, and this casserole proves the point. You can use any firm-fleshed white fish instead of cod – made with turbot, this dish is superb. I like to serve it with creamy mashed potatoes and a green vegetable.

Serves 6
900 g (2 lb) cod, filleted and cut into chunks about 2.5 cm (1 in) in
  size
5–6 tbsp oil
25 g (1 oz) butter
2 large or 3 medium onions, skinned and thinly sliced
3 rashers streaky bacon, coarsely chopped
3 eating apples – Granny Smith's are ideal – peeled, cored and
  chopped
2 tbsp seasoned flour
575 ml (1 pt) dry cider
275 ml (½ pt) water (or stock made from boiling the skin and bones
  of the cod with an onion)
chopped parsley to garnish (optional)

Roll the pieces of fish in the seasoned flour and put to one side.

Heat 3 tablespoons of the oil with the butter in a casserole and add the onion. Cook for about 3 minutes, then add the bacon and cook for a further 5 minutes, stirring occasionally so that they cook evenly. Add the apple and cook for a further couple of minutes. Stir in 1 tablespoon of the seasoned flour, cook for a minute or two longer, then stir in the cider and water or fish stock, stirring until the sauce boils. (You can do all this several hours in advance.)

About 30 minutes before you want to serve the casserole, heat about 2 tablespoons of oil in a frying pan, and gently fry the pieces of cod for barely 2 minutes. Then add them to the casserole, cover and bake in a moderate oven (180°C, 350°F, gas 4) for 20–25 minutes.

Serve hot, with a dusting of chopped parsley if you like.

107 Cod Provençale

Like many dishes, this can be made with any firm-fleshed white fish. There is no thickening agent – the garlicky tomato sauce thickens by reducing as it simmers. I like to serve this with brown rice, and a salad with sliced avocado and crisp bacon bits in it.

Serves 6
900 g (2 lb) cod, filleted and cut in pieces about 2.5 cm (1 in) in size
3 tbsp olive oil
2 medium onions, skinned and thinly sliced
700 g (1½ lb) fresh tomatoes, skinned, seeded and chopped; or
  2 × 425 g (15 oz) cans tomatoes, with most of the juice drained
  off
½ tsp sugar
½ tsp salt
1 large garlic clove, finely chopped
freshly ground black pepper
50 g (2 oz) black olives, stoned and chopped
1 tbsp chopped basil and parsley

Heat the oil in a saucepan and add the onions. Cook over a moderate heat for 5 minutes, stirring occasionally to prevent the onions from burning, until soft and transparent. Stir in the tomatoes, sugar, salt, chopped garlic, plenty of pepper and the olives. Simmer this sauce gently, uncovered, for about 20 minutes.

Stir in the pieces of fish, cover the pan and simmer very gently for a further 15 minutes. Then mix in the basil and parsley, pour into a serving dish and serve immediately.

108 Cod, Mushroom and Bacon Kebabs

In this recipe pieces of cod are wrapped in streaky bacon, then pushed on kebab skewers. These should have flattened blades, so the food threaded on to them doesn't turn round, and will cook evenly. You can cook them either under a grill or on a barbecue. Allow about five pieces of bacon-wrapped fish per person.

They are very good served with either Tomato and garlic mayonnaise or Cucumber and herb mayonnaise (rec. 23 and 24).

Serves 6
900 g (2 lb) fillet of cod, cut in pieces about 2.5 cm (1 in) in size
15 rashers of streaky bacon, cut in half widthwise
about 24 button mushrooms
oil for brushing

Wrap each piece of fish in half a bacon rasher and push on to a skewer, with a mushroom in between each piece. I allow about 5 pieces of fish and bacon and 4 mushrooms per skewer. If you are going to grill them, put the skewers on a baking tray, brush the kebabs with oil, and cook under a moderately hot grill for 7–10 minutes, turning them over during cooking time. The bacon should be fairly crisp, so give them a bit longer if necessary.

If you are cooking the kebabs on a barbecue, brush them with oil, lay them on the barbecue, and turn after a couple of minutes' cooking. Give them about 10 minutes' cooking, but turn them frequently.

109 *Hake with Mushrooms, Cream and Soya Sauce*

The texture of hake is very similar to that of cod – indeed a hake is like a long cod, if anything somewhat firmer. This is a luxurious dish, dressing hake up. It can also be made with brill, turbot or halibut fillets.

Serves 6
900 g (2 lb) hake fillets
225 g (8 oz) mushrooms, wiped and sliced
75 g (3 oz) butter
2–3 tsp soya sauce
284 ml (½ pt) single cream
2 tbsp seasoned flour
salt and freshly ground black pepper
finely chopped parsley to garnish (optional)

Melt the butter in a wide, shallow pan and cook the mushrooms for a minute, then remove them to a dish and keep warm.

Cut the fish into chunks about 4 cm (1½ in) in size and roll them in the seasoned flour. Put the chunks into the pan and cook for 2–3 minutes, turning them over several times. Stir in the soya sauce and cream, and season with salt and pepper.

Return the mushrooms to the pan and bring to simmering point. Simmer for 10 minutes, then pour into a warmed serving dish and serve, sprinkled with finely chopped parsley if you like.

110 Invergarry Crab Cakes

I generally prefer eating crab cold, but crab cakes are the exception. They are very good served with either Tartare sauce, or with a homemade Tomato sauce (rec. 26 and 29).

Crab cakes freeze well, for up to 3 months. This quantity makes about 6 large cakes, or more small ones. They are very filling!

Serves 4–6
450 g (1 lb) crabmeat
3 slices brown bread, crusts removed and the bread made into crumbs
2 heaped tbsp mayonnaise
2 rounded tsp English mustard
1 tbsp Worcestershire sauce
oil and butter for frying
For the coating
1 egg, beaten
6 rounded tbsp brown breadcrumbs

Mix together the crabmeat, breadcrumbs, mayonnaise, mustard and Worcestershire sauce until they are well combined. Shape the mixture into cakes about 2 cm (¾ in) thick. This is easier to do if you dip your hands in flour. If you are going to freeze them, put them on a paper plate, wrap well and freeze them at this stage. Thaw for an hour or two before coating and frying them.

To coat, dip each crab cake in the beaten egg and then in the breadcrumbs, and leave on a tray in the fridge for 2–3 hours. Then heat about 4 tablespoons of oil and 50 g (2 oz) of butter in a large frying pan, and fry the crab cakes for 3–5 minutes on each side until they are golden brown. Drain on absorbent paper and serve with a green salad.

111 Baked Plaice with Onions, Tomatoes and White Wine

This is a very good dish for those who are counting calories. I like to serve it with brown rice and a green vegetable, like courgettes, or a green salad.

Serves 6
12 fillets of plaice (or lemon sole)
2 tbsp oil
2 medium onions, skinned and very finely sliced
450 g (1 lb) tomatoes, skinned, seeded and cut in strips
150 ml (¼ pt) white wine
salt and freshly ground black pepper
1 tbsp chopped parsley

Heat the oil in a frying pan and add the onion. Cook for 5–7 minutes, stirring occasionally so that the onions cook evenly, until they are soft and transparent. Add the tomato and wine and season with a pinch of salt and plenty of pepper. Simmer gently for 3–5 minutes.

Butter a shallow ovenproof dish. Roll up the fillets of fish, put them in the dish and pour the tomato mixture over. Cover the dish with a piece of foil and bake in a moderate oven (180°C, 350°F, gas 4) for 30 minutes.

Sprinkle with chopped parsley and serve hot.

112 Tuna Fish in Hot Creamy Mayonnaise Sauce

This sauce sounds rather surprising as you don't often come across a hot sauce which has mayonnaise as one of its ingredients. This is very quick to make, and you can substitute any white fish for the tuna, if you prefer. With tuna fish this recipe is one of those standbys that can be made from the contents of your store cupboard.

Serves 6
2 × 200 g (7 oz) cans tuna fish, drained
50 g (2 oz) butter
50 g (2 oz) flour
1 rounded tbsp curry powder
200 g (7 oz) can evaporated milk
575 ml (1 pt) milk
4 tbsp mayonnaise
2 tbsp lemon juice
50 g (2 oz) Cheddar cheese, grated
4 tbsp breadcrumbs mixed with 2 tbsp chopped parsley

Melt the butter and stir in the flour and curry powder. Cook for a couple of minutes. Then stir in the evaporated milk and the milk, stirring until the sauce boils. Draw the pan off the heat and stir in the mayonnaise, lemon juice and cheese. Add the tuna fish and pour the mixture into a buttered, shallow ovenproof dish. Cover the surface with the breadcrumbs and parsley.

Bake in a moderate oven (190°C, 375°F, gas 5) for 20–25 minutes, until the crumbs are browned and the sauce bubbling.

Serve with baked potatoes and a green salad.

113 Tuna Fish and Pasta Salad

You can use any of the interestingly shaped pastas for this decorative salad. I tend to use shells or bows. You can leave the strips of red pepper raw, but blanching makes them more digestible. The quantity of garlic in the recipe can be altered to suit your personal taste. As I love garlic with a passion, the amount given may be too much for those with a mere liking for garlic!

Serves 6
2 × 200 g (7 oz) cans tuna fish, drained
350 g (12 oz) pasta shells, cooked and drained
2 tbsp oil
4 tbsp mayonnaise
2 tbsp lemon juice
salt and freshly ground black pepper
2 red peppers, seeded, cut in thin strips and blanched in boiling
   water for 2 minutes
2 garlic cloves, skinned and finely chopped
chopped parsley and chives to garnish

Mix together all the above ingredients, breaking the tuna into large flakes but not mashing it. Pile into a serving dish or bowl and sprinkle with chopped chives and parsley.

114 *Fresh Pilchards and Sardines*

The word pilchard brings to mind those canned in tomato sauce, but fresh pilchards, like sardines, are delicious. I think they are best cleaned (don't bother to cut their heads off unless you feel squeamish), put on a baking tray, brushed with melted butter and popped under a grill. They will take about 3 minutes' cooking time per side.

Serve with a lemon wedge and allow about 3 fish per person. They are even better cooked on a barbecue – personally I love the charcoaly taste with all fish.

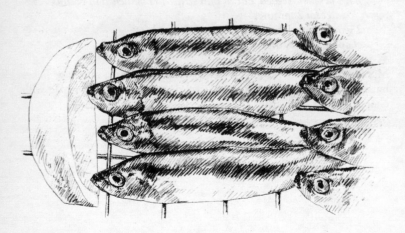

115 Cod with Garlic Butter and Almonds

This dish takes less than 10 minutes to prepare and cook, surely one of my quickest! I like to serve it with sauté potatoes or brown rice and a green vegetable such as broccoli.

Serves 6
900 g (2 lb) cod fillet, cut into 2.5 cm (1 in) pieces
50 g (2 oz) butter and 1 tbsp oil
50 g (2 oz) flaked almonds
1–2 large garlic cloves, finely chopped
salt and freshly ground black pepper
1 tbsp finely chopped parsley

Heat the butter and oil in a large frying pan. Add the cod, almonds and garlic and cook, stirring occasionally, turning the pieces of fish over so that they cook evenly on both sides. Season with a pinch of salt and plenty of pepper. Just before serving sprinkle over the chopped parsley.

116 Spinach, Cod and Cheese Roulade

This is one of those useful dishes where the vegetables and fish are all together in one – I generally serve garlic-buttered warm brown rolls with it. Sometimes I make it with smoked haddock as the filling, and for a much more ritzy dish you can substitute prawns.

Serves 6–8
900 g (2 lb) frozen spinach, thawed and with as much water squeezed out as possible
125 g (4 oz) butter
4 eggs, separated
salt and freshly ground black pepper
freshly grated nutmeg
700 g (1½ lb) cod
0.8 litre (1½ pt) milk
1 onion, skinned
2 tbsp flour
125 g (4 oz) grated cheese
1 tsp English mustard

Line a Swiss roll tin measuring about 30 × 35 cm (12 × 14 in) with a piece of baking paper (siliconized greaseproof paper). Put the spinach into a food processor or liquidizer with 25 g (1 oz) of the butter and whiz, adding the egg yolks one by one. Season with salt, pepper and nutmeg. Then whisk the egg whites until they are very stiff and, using a metal spoon, fold them quickly but thoroughly into the spinach mixture. Pour into the lined tin, smoothing it evenly. Bake in a moderate oven (180°C, 350°F, gas 4) for 25 minutes until firm to the touch.

Meanwhile cook the fish. Put it in a saucepan with the milk and onion, place over moderate heat and bring the milk slowly to the boil. Simmer gently for 2 minutes, then draw the pan off the heat and let the fish cool in the milk for 10 minutes or so.

Melt the remaining butter in a saucepan and stir in the flour. Cook for a minute or two, then gradually add the milk the fish cooked in, stirring all the time, until the sauce boils. Stir in all but a spoonful of the grated cheese and all the mustard. Flake the cooked fish into the cheese sauce, picking out any bones.

Put a fresh piece of baking paper on a work surface and sprinkle the remaining grated cheese over it. Tip the cooked roulade face down on to the paper and carefully peel the old paper off its back. Spread the fish and cheese sauce over the surface. Place a large serving dish close beside the roulade, roll it up lengthwise and slip it on to the dish. Serve hot – it will keep warm for about 20 minutes without spoiling.

117 Baked Sole with Capers and Lemon Juice

This is a marvellous dish for slimmers, served with a green vegetable or mixed salad, and it is equally good made with haddock.

Serves 4
8 fillets of sole or haddock
1 jar of capers – how many you use depends on your liking for them
juice of 1 large lemon
salt and freshly ground black pepper
chopped parsley to garnish

Butter a shallow ovenproof dish liberally. Put about a teaspoonful of capers on each fish fillet and roll the fillet up. Put the rolls into the buttered dish. Season with salt and pepper and pour the lemon juice over. Cover the dish with a piece of foil and bake in a moderate oven (180°C, 350°F, gas 4) for 30–35 minutes – the fish should flake easily when it is cooked.

Sprinkle with chopped parsley before serving.

118 John Dory Fillets Baked with Mushrooms and Sherry

John Dory is quite an expensive fish to buy, for you can only eat about one third of it, the other two-thirds being its huge and sternly ugly head and its guts. But in taste it is on a par with sole or turbot.

Serves 6
about 700 g (1½ lb) filleted fish
50 g (2 oz) butter and 2 tbsp oil
2 medium onions, skinned and very thinly sliced
450 g (1 lb) button mushrooms, wiped and sliced
grated nutmeg
salt and freshly ground black pepper
1 sherry glass medium sherry
extra butter to finish

Heat the butter and oil in a frying pan and add the onion. Cook over a moderate heat until it is soft and transparent, then add the mushrooms, nutmeg, salt and pepper and sherry. Cook for just a minute, then pour the lot into an ovenproof dish.

Put in the fish fillets and dot them with bits of butter. Cover the dish with its lid or a piece of foil. Bake in a moderate oven (190°C, 375°F, gas 5) for about 30 minutes. Lift the foil and see if the fish is cooked; give it another 5 minutes if necessary.

119 Baked Bream with Garlic and Peppers

This can be made equally well using fillets of brill, halibut or turbot. The fish is baked on top of a pre-cooked mixture of onions, garlic and red and yellow peppers.

Serves 6
900 g (2 lb) fillets of bream
5 tbsp olive oil
2 medium onions, skinned and thinly sliced
2 red and 2 yellow peppers, seeded, halved and thinly sliced
salt and freshly ground black pepper

Heat the olive oil in a wide, shallow pan, or a frying pan, and add the onion. Cook for 3–5 minutes, until the onion is soft and transparent. Then add the peppers, season with salt and plenty of pepper and cook over a low heat for about 30 minutes, stirring from time to time.

Pour the mixture into a shallow, ovenproof dish and arrange the fish fillets on top, pushing them down into it. Cover the dish with foil and bake in a moderate oven (190°C, 375°F, gas 5) for 30 minutes.

This is delicious served with creamy mashed potatoes and fresh garden peas.

120 *Lemon Baked Red Mullet*

Small mullet are best, I think, just brushed with melted butter and put under a grill for about 3 minutes each side. But larger ones are good baked on a bed of lemon and parsley, wrapped in a foil parcel. Try and leave the liver in each fish when you clean it – or ask the fishmonger to do so for you.

Serves 4
4 × 225 g (8 oz) mullet cleaned
2 lemons, thinly sliced
a few parsley sprigs
salt and freshly ground black pepper
butter for greasing
lemon wedges to serve

Butter 4 large pieces of foil, and lay about 3 slices of lemon in the middle of each. Put the mullet on top. Add a parsley sprig and season with salt and pepper. Wrap the parcels up and put them on a baking tray. Bake in a moderate oven (190°C, 375°F, gas 5) for 20 minutes.
　　Serve each fish with a lemon wedge beside it.

121 Baked Bass with Lemon and Parsley Stuffing

In this recipe the fish has slivers of garlic pushed into slits in its flesh, and the stuffing is very lemony – a lovely combination. It is very good served with Horseradish and parsley sauce messine (rec. 35).

Serves 6
1 × 1.4 kg (3 lb) bass (or 2 smaller ones), cleaned and descaled
50 g (2 oz) butter
1 small onion, skinned and very finely chopped
75 g (3 oz) fresh breadcrumbs – brown or white
grated rind of 2 lemons, juice of 1 lemon
2 tbsp finely chopped parsley
salt and freshly ground black pepper
2 garlic cloves, skinned and slivered

Melt the butter in a saucepan and add the onion. Cook for 3–5 minutes, stirring occasionally, until the onion is soft and transparent. Take the pan off the heat and stir in the breadcrumbs, lemon rind, parsley, salt and plenty of pepper.

Stuff the bass with this stuffing. Butter a large piece of foil and put the stuffed bass on it. Cut little slashes in its flesh and push a sliver of garlic into each. Wrap the fish up in the foil and put the parcel on a baking tray. Bake in a moderate oven (180°C, 350°F, gas 4) for 30 minutes.

Unwrap the foil and stick a knife into the fish to see if it is cooked. If you think it needs a bit longer, wrap it up again and pop it back in the oven for 5 minutes.

122 Bass Baked with Tomato and Fennel

This dish is for those who love the aniseed-like flavour of fennel. Bass is good cut into steaks and grilled, or baked with a tasty stuffing. In this recipe the fish is laid whole on pre-cooked vegetables and baked.

Serves 6
1 × 1.4 kg (3 lb) bass (or 2 smaller ones), cleaned and descaled
4 tbsp olive oil
1 large onion, skinned and cut into thin rings
2 heads of fennel, thinly sliced
450 g (1 lb) tomatoes, skinned, seeded and quartered
salt and freshly ground black pepper
225 ml (8 fl oz) dry vermouth

Heat the olive oil in a large, heavy casserole which has a lid. Add the onion and cook for about 5 minutes, stirring occasionally, until it is soft and transparent. Add the fennel, cook for a further 5 minutes, then add the tomatoes, salt, plenty of pepper and the vermouth. Simmer, uncovered, for 15 minutes.

Then lay the bass on top of the vegetables and spoon some of them over it. Cover the casserole and bake in a moderate oven (190°C, 375°F, gas 5) for 30 minutes.

M·A·I·N C·O·U·R·S·E·S F·O·R S·P·E·C·I·A·L O·C·C·A·S·I·O·N·S

Lobster
Poached Salmon
Shellfish, Cream and Brandy Stew
Shrimp Puff Pie
Crab Cream Tart
Crab Soufflé
Barbecued Salmon
Salmon Filleted and Baked, John Tovey
Salmon Steaks
Salmon and Dill Cream Tart
Salmon en Croûte
Coulibiac of Salmon
Salmon Heckfield
Shark or Swordfish Steaks
Fish and Bacon Kebabs
Devilled Seafood
Shellfish in Curried Garlic Mayonnaise
Trout with Almonds and Cream
Scallops with White Wine and Cheese Sauce
Halibut or Turbot Salad
Prawn and Orange Salad
Mixed Fish Mayonnaise
Poached Monkfish with Leek and Vermouth Sauce

123 *Lobster*

One of the most fascinating things about lobsters is the way they change colour. Uncooked they are a handsome navy blue; cooked they transform to a rich coral red. A lobster weighing about 450 g (1 lb) is ample for one person. Whether you prefer them hot, as does Godfrey, or cold, like me, they should be served with the simplest of accompaniments, so that their flavour and succulent texture can be fully appreciated.

To cook – presuming you have several lobsters – put several pints of water into a large saucepan which has a tightly fitting lid. Bring the water to the boil, and put in the live lobsters. (If you prefer, ask your fishmonger to kill the lobsters for you.) Cover and bring the water back to the boil. Boil for 15–20 minutes, then, using tongs, take the cooked lobsters out of the water and put them on a baking tray.

If you are going to serve them hot, split them down the middle, taking out the bag in the head, and the intestine – the dark thread running down the tail. Serve with melted butter with lemon juice and chopped chives in it.

If the lobsters are to be served cold don't split them until they are cold. Serve with either plain mayonnaise, or with Cucumber and herb mayonnaise (rec. 24). Tartare sauce (rec. 26) is also very good with cold lobster.

124 *Poached Salmon*

Where we live, and I should think in a great many other parts of the British Isles, the term poached salmon could equally well refer to the method of procuring the salmon as to the method of cooking it. The salmon on the menu at Kinloch, I must hasten to add, do not arrive at the back door at dead of night, but are bought legitimately. We buy farmed salmon when wild are unobtainable, from the excellent salmon farm owned by Ian Anderson at Strathaird. But my preference is for wild salmon, and these we buy from various enterprising individuals who rent the local salmon rights and keep us supplied for many weeks.

We use a fish kettle to poach whole fish but they are so expensive to buy now that few people own them, except those lucky enough to have inherited one. This is how I used to cook salmon when I didn't have access to a fish kettle. Gut the fish and weigh it. Allow 20 minutes per 450 g (1 lb). Take a piece of foil large enough to wrap the fish in, and lay it on the work surface. Smear butter liberally over it and put a few sprigs of parsley and slices of lemon on top. Lay the fish on this, and put a few more sprigs of parsley, 3–4 slices of lemon and a generous lump of butter inside the fish. Put more parsley sprigs and a further couple of slices of lemon on top and wrap into a parcel with the foil.

Put the fish in a roasting tin half-filled with water. Put the tin in a moderate oven (180°C, 350°F, gas 4) for 15 minutes, then lower the heat to 130°C (250°F, gas ½). For a fish weighing about 3.6 kg (8 lb) take it out of the oven after 2 hours and unwrap to see if it is cooked. Ease up the skin with 2 forks – if it lifts up readily the fish is cooked. The fish probably won't be quite ready at this stage, but it is much better to test too soon rather than too late, as if overcooked it will be dry, and no amount of hollandaise or mayonnaise will redeem it.

As soon as it is cooked remove it from the oven. If you are going to serve it cold let it cool in the foil. If it is to be served hot unwrap the foil parcel, take the skin off the side of salmon uppermost, then slide the salmon, turning it over at the same time, on to a warmed flat serving dish and take the skin off the other side. Have a fresh piece of buttered foil ready to cover the salmon. Keep the fish warm in a cool oven until you are ready to serve it.

A 3.6 kg (8 lb) fish will serve about 10–12 people – salmon is very filling. If you have any left over there are numerous ways of using it up, for example: Potted salmon with orange and walnuts (rec. 56), Kedgeree (rec. 15) or Salmon and parsley soup (rec. 2).

125 Shellfish, Cream and Brandy Stew

This is a most luxurious dish, fit for a very special occasion. But it is extremely quick to make as all the shellfish added to the sauce are already cooked. (You can vary the quantities and types of shellfish to suit your preferences and local availability.) The only thing to beware of is not to overcook the shellfish; just heat them through in the sauce before serving. If simmered for any length of time they will become tough.

After serving this as a main course, a light fruity dessert is ideal, perhaps a sorbet, but nothing too rich.

Serves 6–8
1 cooked lobster, weighing about 700 g (1½ lb), flesh cut into chunks
8 large scallops, cooked and cut in half
225 g (8 oz) cooked, shelled prawns
225 g (8 oz) white crabmeat
575 ml (1 pt) mussels, measured in their shells, cooked, then taken out of their shells (discard any which remain shut)
For the sauce
75 g (3 oz) butter
2 medium onions, skinned and finely chopped
2 tsp curry powder
1 rounded tbsp flour
284 ml (½ pt) double cream
6 tbsp brandy
salt and freshly ground black pepper
1 heaped tbsp finely chopped parsley

First make the sauce. Melt the butter in a large saucepan. Add the onion and cook for 5 minutes until it is soft and transparent. Stir in the curry powder and flour and cook for a further couple of minutes. Then pour in the cream, stirring all the time until the sauce is simmering gently. Take the pan off the heat and stir in the brandy. Add the shellfish, reheat, stirring carefully so as not to break them up, until the sauce is just barely simmering once more. Tip the contents of the saucepan into a warmed serving dish, sprinkle with the chopped parsley and serve.

This is good accompanied by rice, and a good mixed salad served separately.

126 *Shrimp Puff Pie*

I like this best of all when it is made with the tiny pink Morecambe Bay shrimps, which have a delicate, slightly peppery taste. The only spice needed in the sauce is a grating of nutmeg. The puff pastry on top of the pie means that you don't need potatoes or rice; simply serve with, say, carrots with a lemon glaze, and courgettes sliced thinly and cooked in olive oil and garlic.

Serves 8
0.8 litre (1½ pt) milk
1 small onion, skinned and halved
1 stick of celery, halved
1 blade of mace
a few black peppercorns
50 g (2 oz) butter
50 g (2 oz) flour
900 g (2 lb) shrimps
freshly grated nutmeg
450 g (1 lb) puff pastry
1 egg, beaten

Put the milk, onion, celery, mace and peppercorns in a saucepan over a gentle heat. Bring slowly to the boil, then draw the pan off the heat and leave to infuse for 30 minutes or so. Then strain the milk into a jug, ready for making into the sauce.

Melt the butter in a saucepan and stir in the flour. Cook for a couple of minutes, then stir in the milk, stirring all the time until the sauce boils. Remove the pan from the heat and stir in the shrimps. Season with nutmeg. Pour into a greased pie dish.

Flour a working surface and roll out the pastry. Dampen the rim of the pie dish and cover the pie neatly. Cut 4–5 little slashes in the surface of the pie and decorate it with pastry trimmings. Brush with beaten egg. Bake in a hot oven (200°C, 400°F, g   6) for 35 minutes, or until the pastry is well risen and golden brown.

127 Crab Cream Tart

My sister Liv makes stunning crab quiches, but as I think the word quiche is much over-used, here at Kinloch we call them cream tarts. Whatever you call them, they make a superb lunch or supper dish, served with warm brown rolls and a good salad, green or mixed.

Serves 6–8
Shortcrust pastry to line a flan dish about 25 cm (10 in) in diameter. I make my pastry like this:
125 g (4 oz) butter, hard from the fridge, cut in bits into a food processor
175 g (6 oz) flour
2 level tsp icing sugar
For the filling
450 g (1 lb) crabmeat
1 tbsp snipped chives
2 eggs and 3 yolks
284 ml (½ pt) single cream or cream and milk mixed
salt and freshly ground black pepper
red pepper sauce (Tabasco)
finely chopped parsley

All the pastry ingredients are whizzed in a food processor until the mixture is like fine crumbs. If you don't have a food processor, make the pastry as crumb-like as possible by cutting the butter into the mixture with a sharp knife and rubbing it in with your fingers. Then pat and press this round the insides of the flan dish, and put the dish in the fridge for at least half an hour, longer if possible, then bake blind in a moderate oven (180°C, 350°F, gas 4), for 20–25 minutes, until the pastry is golden brown and cooked. Cool.

Beat together the eggs and yolks, and stir in the crabmeat, chives and cream; season with a good dash of red pepper sauce, a pinch of salt and pepper. Pour this into the cooked pastry shell and bake in a moderate oven (180°C, 350°F, gas 4) for about 15–20 minutes, until the filling is just firm to the touch.

Serve either hot or cold, with the surface of the tart dusted with parsley.

128 Crab Soufflé

As with all soufflés this has to be eaten immediately it comes out of the oven. There can be no sadder sight than that of a slowly sinking soufflé!

Serves 6
225 g (8 oz) crabmeat
50 g (2 oz) butter
50 g (2 oz) flour
275 ml (½ pt) milk
3 tbsp medium dry sherry
50 g (2 oz) grated cheese
salt and freshly ground black pepper
red pepper sauce (Tabasco)
5 eggs, separated

Butter a large soufflé dish, about 25 cm (10 in) in diameter.

Melt the butter in a saucepan and stir in the flour. Cook for a couple of minutes, then gradually add the milk, stirring all the time, until the sauce boils. Draw the saucepan off the heat and stir in the sherry and grated cheese. Season with a pinch of salt, pepper and a dash of Tabasco. Beat in the egg yolks one by one and lastly stir in the crabmeat.

Whisk the egg whites until they are very stiff and, using a metal spoon, fold them quickly but thoroughly into the crab sauce mixture. Pour this into the buttered soufflé dish and bake in a hot oven (200°C, 400°F, gas 6) for 35–40 minutes.

Serve at once with a salad and warm brown rolls.

129 *Barbecued Salmon*

My mother was very sceptical when I told her that I intended to barbecue the salmon for dinner that evening, but she declared it to be the best salmon she had ever eaten – praise indeed. Although the salmon is wrapped in foil to be cooked, inevitably during cooking it gets punctured in several places, and the charcoal flavour permeates the fish. Although delectable, it is not smart dinner-party material, but it is ideal for an informal supper or lunch party. The cooking time depends on the heat and size of the barbecue but check each side after 20–25 minutes.

I like to serve barbecued salmon with Tomato and garlic mayonnaise (rec. 23) or Cucumber and herb mayonnaise (rec. 24), new potatoes and a couple of good salads, like tomato and melon salad with mint vinaigrette, and a good mixed green salad.

130 *Salmon Filleted and Baked, John Tovey*

I can claim no credit for thinking up this way of cooking salmon, which we think here at Kinloch is definitely the best method when it is to be eaten hot (with the exception of barbecuing, which is equally good but quite different). I had eaten salmon at Miller Howe, John Tovey's superb hotel and restaurant high above Lake Windermere, and I had enjoyed it very much, but it was not until I went to a demonstration of cooking given by John in Inverness that I realized that what I had eaten was the filleted salmon he was demonstrating. Served with hollandaise sauce it is divine, and it is the way we always cook and serve salmon for our guests.

Salmon is rich (richer still when served with hollandaise) and you don't need to give people enormous pieces. From a whole fish weighing about 4 kg (9 lb), when gutted, filleted and skinned we get about 8–10 portions. For the details of gutting, cleaning, filleting, etc., please look at the first chapter in this book. The first time you fillet a salmon it takes a while, and it is a job that just can't be hurried, but, given a really sharp knife, it isn't at all arduous.

Cut the fillets in the required number of pieces and put them on a baking tray. Put a 10–25 g (½–1 oz) lump of butter on each piece of salmon, don't season the fish at all, and bake in a moderately hot oven (200°C, 400°F, gas 6) for 5 minutes. Take them out of the oven and serve immediately, with Hollandaise sauce (rec. 28).

131 Salmon Steaks

I used to despise salmon steaks, because to me they were synonymous with salmon at its worst – overcooked, dry and chewy. I was so wrong, because if salmon steaks are properly and gently cooked they are marvellous.

Serves 4
4 salmon steaks
75 g (3 oz) butter, melted

Put the steaks on a baking tray. Brush them with some of the melted butter and put the tray under a moderately hot grill. Cook for a couple of minutes, then brush again with butter and put back under the grill for a further couple of minutes. Then turn the steaks over, brush with butter, and repeat the cooking process on this side.

Before serving stick the prongs of a fork down into the edge of the skin on each steak, and turn the fork so that the skin wraps itself round the fork as it peels off the steak – this is an easy way of skinning the steaks, which are much nicer served without their skin.

Serve with either Hollandaise sauce (rec. 28) or with Cream, lemon and chive sauce (rec. 30).

132 Salmon and Dill Cream Tart

I used to make this tart using left-over cooked salmon. It was good, but the salmon was invariably dry – because it was overcooked. Then I tried making it with raw salmon, cut into chunks, and the result was superb. It is so simple, and can be the first course for a dinner party, the main course for a lunch party, or the main part of an elegant picnic.

Serves 6–8
For the pastry
125 g (4 oz) butter, hard from the fridge, cut in bits
175 g (6 oz) flour
2 tsp icing sugar
1 tsp salt
freshly ground black pepper
For the filling
450 g (1 lb) fresh salmon
2 eggs
2 egg yolks
575 ml (1 pt) single cream, or milk and cream mixed
salt and freshly ground black pepper
a few sprigs of dill

Put all the pastry ingredients into a food processor and whiz until the mixture is like fine breadcrumbs. If you don't have a food processor, cut the butter into the mixture with a sharp knife and rub it in with your fingers to make the pastry more crumb-like. Then pat this around the sides and bottom of a flan dish measuring about 20 cm (8 in) in diameter. Put the flan dish in the fridge for at least 30 minutes, longer if possible, then bake in a moderate oven (180°C, 350°F, gas 4) for about 30 minutes, or until the pastry is evenly cooked and golden brown.

Cut the salmon into 2.5 cm (1 in) cubes. Arrange them evenly over the cooked pastry. Beat together the eggs, yolks, cream, salt and pepper, and pour the mixture over the salmon. Tear the dill into bits and scatter over the surface. Bake in a low oven (170°C, 325°F, gas 3) for 30 minutes, until the filling is just set to the touch.

133 Salmon en Croûte

This is an elaborate dish, worthy of a special-occasion dinner or lunch party. The filleted salmon is laid on a bed of onions, parsley and cucumber inside a puff pastry parcel and baked. Serve it with Cream, lemon and chive sauce (rec. 30).

Serves 6–8
A salmon weighing about 4 kg (9 lb) skinned and filleted
1 cucumber
2 onions, skinned and finely chopped
225 ml (8 fl oz) dry white wine
700 g (1½ lb) puff pastry
1 large bunch of parsley, finely chopped
1 egg, beaten

Peel the cucumber, halve it and scoop out the seeds. Dice the flesh, put it in a bowl and sprinkle with salt. Leave for at least 30 minutes, then drain the juices away, rinse the cucumber and pat it dry.

Put the onion into a saucepan with the wine, and, over a moderate heat, simmer until the wine has reduced so much that it has almost disappeared, leaving the onions soft and cooked. This takes about 30 minutes.

Meanwhile roll out the pastry and divide it in half.

When the onions are cooked mix them with the parsley and prepared cucumber. Spread this over the surface of one piece of pastry which you have placed on a baking tray and lay the salmon on top, tucking the tail end under so that you have about the same thickness of salmon both ends. Cover with the other piece of pastry, brush the edges with beaten egg, and fold one edge over the other and crimp together so that they form a neat oblong parcel. Brush the surface with beaten egg, and cut 3 diagonal slashes in the top. Bake in a moderately hot oven (200°C, 400°F, gas 6) for 30–35 minutes.

Serve hot, cut in slices, with the sauce handed separately.

You can prepare salmon en croûte right up to the point where you are ready to pop it into the oven well ahead of time – say in the morning for dinner that evening. Keep it in the fridge until about an hour before cooking.

134 Coulibiac of Salmon

A couple of years ago Coulibiac – salmon baked in puff pastry – was a recipe which sprang to the eye from countless cookery columns. It is one which deserves to stay in fashion, because it is so good, also convenient, because it can be made up to the baking stage in the morning, then popped in the oven in time for dinner. It is generally made with salmon, but I have seen a recipe using tuna fish.

Serves 6–8
900 g (2 lb) fresh salmon
50 g (2 oz) butter
1 large onion, skinned and finely chopped
225 g (8 oz) button mushrooms, chopped
2 hard-boiled eggs, shelled and chopped
2 tbsp finely chopped parsley
salt and freshly ground black pepper
700 g (1½ lb) puff pastry
50 g (2 oz) rice, boiled until tender in chicken stock
1 egg, beaten

Cut the salmon into small chunks, about 1 cm (½ in) in size.

Melt the butter and cook the onion in it for about 5 minutes until it is soft and transparent. Then add the mushrooms, and cook for another minute or two. Set aside.

Mix together the hard-boiled eggs and parsley. Season with salt and pepper.

Put a piece of baking paper on a baking tray. Divide the pastry in half, and roll out one piece into a rectangle about 35 × 25 cm (14 × 10 in). Lay this on the baking tray. Cover it with the cooked, drained rice, leaving a margin of about 4 cm (1½ in) round the edges. Next arrange the chunks of salmon on the rice. Follow this with the hard-boiled eggs and parsley mixture, and lastly the mushroom and onion mixture.

Roll out the other piece of pastry. Brush the margin of the first piece with beaten egg, and put the second piece on top. Press the edges together firmly and trim off any bits which overhang. Slash 5–6 times diagonally across the top of the pastry parcel, and brush it all over with beaten egg.

Bake in a moderately hot oven (200°C, 400°F, gas 6), for 35–40 minutes. Serve either hot or cold – I prefer it cold.

135 *Salmon Heckfield*

This dish, named after the house in which it originated, is composed of a set, creamy, mousse-like mixture, with a puff pastry top, and is served with Hollandaise sauce. It is extraordinary because it is rare to find something so luxurious made of left-overs. Having said that, it is so good that if you don't happen to have a pound of cooked salmon left over from anything, it is worth while buying it raw and cooking it. (If you do use raw salmon, cook it by the John Tovey method given in recipe 130.)

Serves 6
450 g (1 lb) cooked salmon, flaked from its skin and bones
4 egg whites
½ tsp salt
284 ml (½ pt) double cream
225 g (8 oz) puff pastry
1 egg, beaten

Whisk the egg whites with a fork until they are broken but not frothy. Put the salmon and salt into a food processor or liquidizer and whiz, adding the cream, until you have a smooth purée. Then whiz in the whites. Put the mixture into a pie dish, and put into the fridge for an hour to chill thoroughly.

Roll out the pastry, and cover the surface of the pie with it, crimping the edges neatly. Brush with beaten egg, and cut 2 slashes in the top. Bake in a hot oven (200°C, 400°F, gas 6) for 25–30 minutes, until the pastry is golden brown and puffed.

Serve with Hollandaise sauce (rec. 28).

136 *Shark or Swordfish Steaks*

Fresh tuna fish, shark and swordfish are unlike such fish as haddock, sole or plaice in that they are really meaty. Their flesh has a much firmer texture. They have a tendency to be dry, due to overcooking at too high a temperature, so I like to simmer the steaks, having first sealed them in hot olive oil, in a good tomato sauce. This helps to keep them moist.

They are good served with noodles or any sort of pasta, tossed in a little cream and freshly grated Parmesan cheese.

Serves 6
6 shark, swordfish or tuna steaks
4 tbsp olive oil
1 garlic clove, skinned and finely chopped
Fresh tomato sauce (rec. 29)

Heat the oil in a frying pan and cook the fish steaks for about a minute on each side. Put them into a large, shallow ovenproof dish. Pour the tomato sauce over the steaks and cover with foil. Bake in a moderate oven (180°C, 350°F, gas 4) for 45–50 minutes.

After 30 minutes have a look under the foil to make sure that the tomato sauce is just simmering around the steaks. This dish will keep warm satisfactorily for about 30 minutes before serving.

137 Fish and Bacon Kebabs

Any firm-textured white fish makes perfect kebabs. I use turbot, but halibut or monkfish are both excellent. I like to barbecue kebabs, but they are very good grilled. If you are grilling them, they need about 10 minutes with frequent turning as they cook. Use proper flat-bladed kebab skewers to ensure they cook evenly.

I like to serve fish kebabs with Tomato and garlic mayonnaise, or with Curried garlic mayonnaise (rec. 23 and 25). With lots of garlic bread and a couple of good salads they make an excellent meal.

Serves 6
900 g (2 lb) turbot or other firm-textured white fish
15 streaky bacon rashers, cut in half widthways

Cut the turbot into chunks – I allow 5 pieces per person. Wrap each chunk of fish in half a streaky bacon rasher and push them on to the skewers. Cook them for about 20 minutes on a barbecue, turning several times during the cooking time so that they cook evenly.

138 Devilled Seafood

The ingredients in this recipe sound odd, I know, but please don't be put off by them, even though your eyebrows are bound to rise as you read down the list – evaporated milk and beef consommé combined with fish? But the end result really is delicious, and is always greatly enjoyed by our guests at Kinloch, judging not only by their comments, but also by their empty plates. It is an American recipe, which was given to my mother way back in the fifties. This is an ideal dish for a buffet party.

Serves 8
900 g (2 lb) haddock or similar white fish
milk and water as required
450 g (1 lb) shellfish (prawns, scallops, crab)
225 g (8 oz) butter
9 rounded tbsp flour
325 ml (12 fl oz) milk
225 ml (8 fl oz) evaporated milk
225 ml (8 fl oz) beef consommé
1 tbsp lemon juice
1 tbsp Worcestershire sauce
4 tbsp tomato ketchup
1 tbsp horseradish
1 garlic clove, skinned and finely chopped
1 rounded tsp English mustard
1 tsp salt
1 tsp soya sauce
a dash of red pepper sauce (Tabasco)
4 rounded tbsp finely chopped parsley
225 ml (8 fl oz) sherry
breadcrumbs and extra butter to finish

Put the haddock in a saucepan with milk and water to cover. Bring slowly to the boil, then remove from the heat and cool. When the fish is cool enough to handle, flake the flesh from the bones and skin.

Melt the butter in a saucepan. Stir in the flour and cook for a couple of minutes. Gradually add all the other ingredients, stirring until the sauce boils. (If it is too stiff for your liking add more milk.) When it has boiled, remove the saucepan from the heat and stir in the flaked fish and the shellfish. Butter an ovenproof dish and pour the devilled seafood into it. Sprinkle the breadcrumbs over the surface and dot with butter. Put the dish under a hot grill to brown the breadcrumbs. Serve with rice and a green salad.

139 Shellfish in Curried Garlic Mayonnaise

This wonderful, rich dish makes a luxurious main course for a very special occasion in the summer. Because it is so rich it should be followed by a fruit dessert – perhaps a raspberry and lemon sorbet with fresh raspberries, or an elderflower sorbet with fresh strawberries.

Serves 6–8
12 large scallops
dry white wine for cooking
450 g (1 lb) crabmeat
450 g (1 lb) shelled, cooked prawns
Curried garlic mayonnaise (rec. 25)

Poach the scallops in a mixture of wine and water for 3–4 minutes, then cool and drain them. Cut each scallop into 3 pieces.

Fold all the shellfish into the mayonnaise and pile the mixture on to a large flat serving platter. I like to arrange cooked brown rice around the fish, and serve it with a tomato salad.

140 Trout with Almonds and Cream

Good rainbow trout, from fish farms, are now widely available. This is a very easy and quick dish to prepare, therefore ideal for a special dinner or lunch at a busy time.

Serves 6
6 rainbow trout, cleaned but with heads and tails left on
75 g (3 oz) flaked almonds
284 ml (½ pt) double cream
salt and freshly ground black pepper
50 g (2 oz) butter
1 tbsp oil
chopped chives (optional)

Put the almonds in a saucepan over a moderate heat and brown them, shaking the saucepan to stop them from burning. Then, when they are fairly evenly toasted, pour on the cream, and simmer for 3–5 minutes. Season with salt and pepper.

Melt the butter and heat the oil in a frying pan until foaming. Fry the trout for 2 minutes on each side. Cut off their heads and tails and remove the skin – actually this usually comes off as they cook, but make sure it is all off. Put the trout on a warmed serving dish and pour the cream and almond sauce over them.

141 *Scallops with White Wine and Cheese Sauce*

I can never make up my mind which way of preparing scallops is my favourite, this way, with cheese and white wine, or the way we call Scallops Kinloch which is in the chapter on first courses. I love both, but then I love scallops.

Serves 6
24 fairly large scallops
575 ml (1 pt) milk
275 ml (½ pt) water
1 onion, skinned and halved
a blade of mace
50 g (2 oz) butter
2 rounded tbsp flour
1 level tsp curry powder
1 sherry glass white wine
75 g (3 oz) Cheddar or Lancashire cheese, grated
freshly ground black pepper

Cut the scallops in half and put them into a saucepan with the milk, water, onion and mace. Bring the liquid slowly to simmering point, then draw the pan off the heat and leave the scallops to cool in the liquid for about 20 minutes.

Meanwhile melt the butter in another saucepan and add the flour and curry powder. Cook for a couple of minutes, then gradually add the strained liquid from the scallops, stirring all the time until the sauce boils. Draw the pan off the heat and stir in the wine and grated cheese. Season with pepper and stir in the cooked scallops. Pour into an ovenproof dish and keep warm until you are ready to serve – don't keep it hot for much more than 20 minutes.

I like to serve this with boiled brown rice and a green vegetable or salad.

142 Halibut or Turbot Salad

Either halibut or turbot is good in this recipe. The fish is cooked in a mixture of wine and water (good fish stock to keep in the deep freeze), cut into chunks served cold in a piquant dressing. I like it best with a green salad and cold brown rice.

Serves 6
700 g (1½ lb) turbot or halibut
1.7 litres (3 pt) water
275 ml (½ pt) dry white wine
2 onions, quartered (leave their skins on)
2 bay leaves
small handful of peppercorns
handful of parsley
For the dressing
1 tbsp lemon juice
2 tbsp white wine vinegar
1 tsp dry mustard
½ tsp salt.
freshly ground black pepper
a few drops of red pepper sauce (Tabasco)
1 small onion, skinned and extremely finely chopped
8 tbsp olive oil

Put the fish into a roasting tin with the water, wine, onion and herbs (reserve some parsley for finishing). Cover the tin with foil and bake in a moderate oven (190°C, 375°F, gas 5) for 35–40 minutes. Lift up the foil and stick a fork into the fish to see if it is cooked; if it isn't, give it another 5 minutes.

Meanwhile, make the dressing. Put all the ingredients into a saucepan, bring to the boil and simmer for 5 minutes.

Cut the cooked fish into chunks and mix it with the hot dressing in a large bowl. Leave to cool completely. Before serving stir in 2 tablespoons of finely chopped parsley; you can also add a tablespoon of chopped chives.

143 Prawn and Orange Salad

This salad looks decorative and tastes delicious. The rosemary in the dressing gives it an unusual flavour and blends perfectly with the prawns and orange.

Serves 4
700 g (1½ lb) large prawns, shelled
4 oranges
For the dressing
½ tsp salt
about 12 grinds of black pepper
½ tsp sugar
a dash of red pepper sauce (Tabasco)
1 small garlic clove, skinned and finely chopped
½ tsp snipped fresh rosemary (or ¼ tsp dried rosemary)
2 celery sticks, washed and very finely sliced
2 tbsp white wine vinegar
5 tbsp olive oil or sunflower oil

Cut the skin and pith off the oranges, and cut the flesh into thin slices. Mix together all the ingredients for the dressing (make it a bit sharper if you like by adding more vinegar).

Arrange the prawns on one side of a serving dish, with the oranges on the other. (If you have a round dish the oranges look very good in the centre, with the prawns around them.) Pour the dressing over the oranges and serve.

144 Mixed Fish Mayonnaise

This makes a perfect main course for a summer lunch or dinner. I like to serve it with the fish in its creamy mayonnaise in the centre of a large flat serving dish, with brown rice round the edges, and wedges of tomato pressed into the rice.

Serves 8
900 g (2 lb) smoked haddock
700 g (1½ lb) white fish fillet
1.1 litres (2 pt) milk
1 onion, skinned
1 blade of mace
142 ml (¼ pt) double cream, whipped
275 ml (½ pt) good mayonnaise
1 rounded tsp curry powder
2 tsp lemon juice
1 heaped tbsp finely chopped parsley and chives, mixed
175 g (6 oz) cooked prawns, shelled
a few cooked mussels
2 hard-boiled eggs, shelled and chopped
2 × 50 g (2 oz) cans anchovy fillets, drained and soaked in milk for a few hours.
275 g (10 oz) brown rice, cooked, cooled and drained
5–6 tomatoes, cut into wedges

Put the smoked and white fish together in a saucepan with the milk, onion and mace and, over a low heat, bring the milk gently to the boil. Simmer for 2 minutes, then remove the pan from the heat. Cool the fish in the milk, then drain. Save the stock and freeze it to use in sauces and soups. Flake the cooled, cooked fish, removing all bones and skin.

Mix together the cream, mayonnaise, curry powder, lemon juice, parsley and chives. Stir in the flaked fish, prawns, mussels and hard-boiled eggs. Arrange in the middle of the serving dish. Drain the anchovy fillets from their milk and pat dry on absorbent paper. Cut each fillet in half lengthwise, and arrange them in a lattice design over the top of the fish mayonnaise. Surround the fish mayonnaise with brown rice, decorate the rice with tomato wedges at evenly spaced intervals.

145 Poached Monkfish with Leek and Vermouth Sauce

Monkfish is usually bought by the tail, which is enough for about 6 people. Only the tail is sold because the rest of the monkfish consists of a huge head, of extreme yet somehow pathetic ugliness. This tail is pure delight to cope with, because with a sharp knife you can slice down each side of the backbone to give you two long, boneless fillets. When cooked the flesh is very firm and succulent, reminiscent of lobster or large Dublin Bay prawns.

Serves 6
1.4 kg (3 lb) monkfish tail
1 carrot, scraped and halved
2 onions, quartered
small handful of black peppercorns
1 bay leaf
handful of parsley
125 ml (4 fl oz) dry white wine
For the sauce
3 large leeks, washed, trimmed and very thinly sliced
the remaining 0.8 litre (1½ pt) fish stock
125 ml (4 fl oz) dry vermouth
salt and freshly ground pepper
175 g (6 oz) butter, cut into 6–8 pieces

Cut the flesh from the backbone of the monkfish and remove the rather slimy membrane which covers it – this doesn't take a minute and isn't nearly so repulsive as it sounds. Put the backbone into a saucepan with about 1.7 litres (3 pt) of water, the carrot, onion, peppercorns, bay leaf and parsley. Cover the pan with a lid and bring to the boil and simmer gently for ½–1 hour.

About 30 minutes before you plan to eat put the monkfish fillets into a roasting tin, and strain half the stock on to it. Add the wine and cover the tin with foil. Bake in a moderate oven (180°C, 350°F, gas 4) for about 30 minutes, or until the fish is cooked – stick a knife into it if you aren't sure, to see if it is at all raw in the middle.

Meanwhile, make the sauce. Put the leeks into a saucepan with the stock, vermouth and seasoning. Simmer, uncovered, over a moderate heat, until the liquid has reduced by half. Then whisk in the butter, a piece at a time, with the pan at the side of the heat to make sure that the stock doesn't boil again. The sauce will thicken to the consistency of pouring cream. Pour it over the cooked monkfish to serve.

S·A·V·O·U·R·I·E·S

Anchovy Sables
Angels on Horseback
Smoked Haddock Beignets
Mushrooms and Kippers on Toast

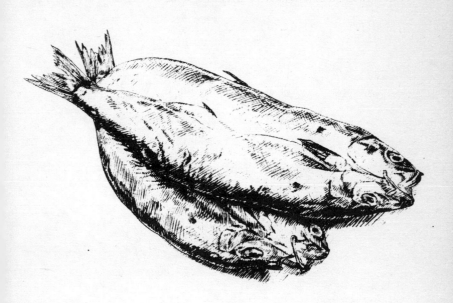

There are still people who would rather finish dinner with a savoury than with a pudding. I am married to just such a person. Godfrey much prefers savouries to sweets, quite the opposite to me. However, from time to time I do make a savoury. The anchovy sables are also good to nibble at the end of a meal *after* the pudding. They are eaten in the fingers, so no more knives and forks are needed. All the savouries can be prepared before dinner starts, with the exception of making the toast, as it is much nicer freshly made.

146 Anchovy Sables

Serves 6
50 g (2 oz) butter
50 g (2 oz) flour
50 g (2 oz) Cheddar cheese, finely grated
½ rounded tsp dry mustard
salt and freshly ground black pepper
50 g (2 oz) can anchovy fillets, drained and soaked in milk
beaten egg

Rub the butter into the flour with your fingertips until the mixture is crumb-like. Mix in the grated cheese, mustard and salt and pepper, until

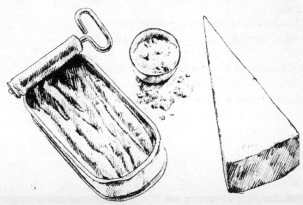

the mixture is blended together into a dough. Roll out the dough about 6 mm (¼ in) thick on a floured surface, and cut into 4 cm (1½ in) rounds or into triangles.

Drain the anchovy fillets on absorbent paper and, with a sharp knife, cut them in half lengthwise. Curl each half in the middle of a pastry shape. Put them on a baking tray and brush with beaten egg. Bake in a moderate oven (190°C, 375°F, gas 5) for about 10 minutes, until they are golden brown.

Leave the sables to cool for 5 minutes before removing them from the baking tray and cooling on a wire rack. If you try to lift them off immediately they will crumble and break.

147 Angels on Horseback

These 'angels' can be grilled before dinner begins, and left in a very cool oven, but leave toasting the 'horses' until just before serving.

Serves 6
12 oysters
12 rashers thinly cut streaky bacon
6 slices of crustless toast, lightly buttered

Wrap each oyster in a bacon rasher. Put them on a baking tray under the grill and cook, turning the little rolls over so that they cook evenly, until the bacon is crisp. Keep warm until ready to serve.

148 *Smoked Haddock Beignets*

These little deep-fried blobs of cheesy choux pastry can be cooked before dinner and kept warm in a cool oven, resting on absorbent paper to absorb any excess oil from the frying, for 2–3 hours. If you like, serve them with Fresh tomato sauce (rec. 29).

Serves 6
*225 g (8 oz) smoked haddock, gently simmered in milk, then cooled,
    and the fish flaked from the bones and skin*
50 g (2 oz) butter
150 ml (¼ pt) water
75 g (3 oz) plain flour, sieved with a pinch of salt
1 rounded tsp dry mustard
3 large eggs
125 g (4 oz) grated Cheddar cheese
freshly ground black pepper
oil for frying

Cut the butter in pieces into the water and put the mixture over a moderately low heat. The butter should melt in the water before it begins to boil. When the first bubbles start to form, draw the pan off the heat and add the sieved flour, all at once. Beat hard until the mixture comes away from the sides of the saucepan. Cool for 5 minutes, then add the mustard and the eggs, one by one, beating well. Stir in the grated cheese, pepper and flaked smoked haddock. (All this can be done in the morning.) To cook, heat oil in a saucepan (or deep-fat fryer) to a depth of about 7.5 cm (3 in). When it is smoking hot, add the fish mixture in teaspoonfuls – I use 2 teaspoons, one with the mixture in and the other to scoop the mixture into the hot oil. Cook about 4 at a time, taking them out of the oil when they are crisp and dark golden-brown. Drain and keep warm until required.

149 *Mushrooms and Kippers on Toast*

The mushrooms in this simple savoury are masked with a creamy sauce containing a small amount of kipper – not too much as kipper last thing at night can be rather repetitive.

Serves 6
6 slices of crustless freshly made toast, lightly buttered
225 g (8 oz) button mushrooms, wiped and sliced
125 g (4 oz) butter
50 g (2 oz) flour
425–575 ml (¾–1 pt) milk
freshly grated nutmeg
salt and freshly ground black pepper
1 kipper, grilled, with the flesh flaked from the bones

Melt half the butter in a saucepan, and when hot add the mushrooms. Cook for just a minute, then scoop them out of the pan on to a dish. (The longer you cook them the more they shrink.) Melt the remaining butter and stir in the flour. Cook for a minute or two, then gradually add enough milk to make a fairly thick sauce, stirring all the time until it boils. Season with nutmeg, a pinch of salt and pepper to taste. Stir in the mushrooms and the flaked cooked kipper.

Put a spoonful of the mushroom and kipper mixture on to the middle of each slice of buttered toast to serve.

I·N·D·E·X

Note: numbers refer to the recipes and not to pages

Delicious Fish